Lynn R. Kahle
Editor

Internet Applications in Euromarketing

Internet Applications in Euromarketing has been co-published simultaneously as *Journal of Euromarketing*, Volume 11, Number 2 2001.

Pre-publication REVIEWS, COMMENTARIES, EVALUATIONS . . .

"COMBINES ACADEMIC RIGOR AND MANAGERIAL USEFULNESS. . . . Shows how marketers can analyze online discussions to learn about consumers by using digital detection theory concepts."

Alain Strazzieri
Doctor of Economics
Professor of Marketing
University of Aix-Marseilles, France

Routledge
Taylor & Francis Group

LONDON AND NEW YORK

More pre-publication
REVIEWS, COMMENTARIES, EVALUATIONS . . .

"**A**DDRESSES IMPORTANT ISSUES related to consumer product involvement, banner advertising and click-through rates, online consumer word-of-mouth influences, and research techniques that can be used to gain insight into consumer reactions to product offerings. The discussions by the chapter authors WILL HELP RESEARCHERS AND MANAGERS think differently and creatively about the problems they confront as well as methods they might use to answer some of their questions."

Curtis P. Haugtvedt
Associate Professor
of Marketing and Logistics
Ohio State University
Past President
Society for Consumer Psychology

"**T**he Internet is a brave new (virtual) world, ripe with possibilities and fraught with pitfalls for companies. This is A USEFUL ADDITION to the library of those intrepid researchers who are charting the unknown territory of this brave new world. Lynn Kahle is a highly respected researcher who has chosen high quality papers to include in this book."

Michael R. Solomon, PhD
Human Sciences Professor
of Consumer Behavior
Auburn University

Internet Applications
in Euromarketing

Internet Applications in Euromarketing has been co-published simultaneously as *Journal of Euromarketing*, Volume 11, Number 2 2001.

The *Journal of Euromarketing* Monographic "Separates"

Below is a list of "separates," which in serials librarianship means a special issue simultaneously published as a special journal issue or double-issue *and* as a "separate" hardbound monograph. (This is a format which we also call a "DocuSerial.")

"Separates" are published because specialized libraries or professionals may wish to purchase a specific thematic issue by itself in a format which can be separately cataloged and shelved, as opposed to purchasing the journal on an on-going basis. Faculty members may also more easily consider a "separate" for classroom adoption.

"Separates" are carefully classified separately with the major book jobbers so that the journal tie-in can be noted on new book order slips to avoid duplicate purchasing.

You may wish to visit Haworth's website at . . .

http://www.HaworthPress.com

. . . to search our online catalog for complete tables of contents of these separates and related publications.

You may also call 1-800-HAWORTH (outside US/Canada: 607-722-5857), or Fax: 1-800-895-0582 (outside US/Canada: 607-771-0012), or e-mail at:

getinfo@haworthpressinc.com

Internet Applications in Euromarketing, edited by Lynn R. Kahle, PhD (Vol. 11, No. 2, 2001) *Examines cutting-edge theory and practice in Internet marketing from North American and European perspectives.*

Foreign Direct Investment and Strategic Alliances in Europe, edited by Hong Liu, PhD (Vol. 10, No. 1, 2001). *Foreign direct investment (FDI) and strategic alliances are among the most popular modes of international market entry and expansion in major markets by multinationals. This book integrates FDI issues with those of strategic alliances to deliver insights into both areas and provides up-close perspectives on specific segments of the European market. It uses case studies, a wide-ranging survey, and the expertise of authorities in the field to shed light on the* when, why, *and* how *of investing and forming alliances in the volatile environment of the European market.*

Global Marketing Co-Operation and Networks, edited by Leo Paul Dana, BA, MBA, PhD (Vol. 9, No. 2, 2000). *"Excellent . . . . well-referenced . . . . very useful. I for one have found it to be current, effective, and useful for developing my own research and teaching materials." (Claudio Vignali, BA, MPhil, DipM, Senior Lecturer, Manchester Metropolitan University, United Kingdom)*

Cross-National Consumer Psychographics, edited by Lynn R. Kahle (Vol. 8, No. 1/2, 1999). *"Cross-National Consumer Psychographics provides marketing professionals and students with data from several applications around the world of the list of values (LOV), so you can consider the implications for understanding consumers cross-culturally. Through this unique book you will find how different countries and different individual consumers may be segmented based on their social values so you can develop the best marketing strategies for your products."*

Newer Insights into Marketing: Cross-Cultural and Cross-National Perspectives, edited by Camille P. Schuster, PhD, and Phil Harris, BA (Hons) (Vol. 7, No. 2, 1999). *This new book analyzes and investigates international marketing strategies to determine effective marketing practices of businesses in the global arena.*

Green Marketing in a Unified Europe, edited by Alma T. Mintu-Wimsatt, PhD, and Héctor R. Lozada, PhD (Vol. 5, No. 3, 1996). *"Takes a well-researched and heartfelt approach to the 3 P's of environmental marketing-preservation, protection, and proactive product development." (Debbie Thorne, PhD, Director, Center for Ethics, The University of Tampa)*

International Joint Ventures in East Asia, edited by Roger Baran, PhD, Yigang Pan, PhD, and Erdener Kaynak, PhD, DSc (Vol. 4, No. 3/4, 1996). *"A valuable resource for anyone interested in joint ventures anywhere in the world." (Sunder Narayanan, PhD, Assistant Professor, School of Business, Columbia University)*

Ethical Issues in International Marketing, edited by Nejdet Delener, PhD (Vol. 4, No. 2, 1995). *"Provides an invaluable education to the reader and encourages the reader to think about important issues that increasingly confront businesspeople in their dealings within a global marketplace." (George V. Priovolos, PhD, CPA, Assistant Professor, Marketing Department, Hagan School of Business, Iona College)*

The Impact of Innovation and Technology in the Global Marketplace, edited by Shaker A. Zahra, PhD, and Abbas J. Ali, PhD (Vol. 3, No. 3/4, 1994). *"The editors have captured the excitement of the present day technological innovations with a wise selection of scholarly articles. Grab this book and read it before it's too late!" (Raymond A. K. Cox, PhD, Professor of Finance, Central Michigan University)*

Internet Applications in Euromarketing

Lynn R. Kahle
Editor

Internet Applications in Euromarketing has been co-published simultaneously as *Journal of Euromarketing*, Volume 11, Number 2 2001.

Routledge
Taylor & Francis Group

LONDON AND NEW YORK

Internet Applications in Euromarketing has been co-published simultaneously as *Journal of Euromarketing*, Volume 11, Number 2 2001.

First published 2001 by The Haworth Press, Inc.

2 Park Square, Milton Park, Abingdon, Oxfordshire OX14 4RN
605 Third Avenue, New York, NY 10017

Routledge is an imprint of the Taylor & Francis Group, an informa business

First issued in hardback 2020

Cover design by Jennifer M. Gaska.

Library of Congress Cataloging-in-Publication Data

Internet applications in Euromarketing / Lynn R. Kahle, editor.
     p. cm.
     "Internet applications in Euromarketing has been co-published simultaneously as Journal of Euromarketing, Volume 11, Number 2 2001."
     Includes bibliographical references and index.
     ISBN 0-7890-2032-7 (hard : alk. paper) - ISBN 0-7890-2033-5 (pbk. : alk. paper)
     1. Internet marketing-European Union countries. 2. Electronic commerce-European Union countries. 3. Consumers-European Union countries-Attitudes. I. Kahle, Lynn R. II. Journal of Euro-marketing.
HF5415.1265 .I56 2002
658.8'4-dc21

          2002013759

ISBN 978-0-7890-2032-1 (hbk)

Indexing, Abstracting & Website/Internet Coverage

This section provides you with a list of major indexing & abstracting services. That is to say, each service began covering this periodical during the year noted in the right column. Most Websites which are listed below have indicated that they will either post, disseminate, compile, archive, cite or alert their own Website users with research-based content from this work. (This list is as current as the copyright date of this publication.)

(continued)

*Special Bibliographic Notes related to special journal issues
(separates) and indexing/abstracting:*

- indexing/abstracting services in this list will also cover material in any "separate" that is co-published simultaneously with Haworth's special thematic journal issue or DocuSerial. Indexing/abstracting usually covers material at the article/chapter level.
- monographic co-editions are intended for either non-subscribers or libraries which intend to purchase a second copy for their circulating collections.
- monographic co-editions are reported to all jobbers/wholesalers/approval plans. The source journal is listed as the "series" to assist the prevention of duplicate purchasing in the same manner utilized for books-in-series.
- to facilitate user/access services all indexing/abstracting services are encouraged to utilize the co-indexing entry note indicated at the bottom of the first page of each article/chapter/contribution.
- this is intended to assist a library user of any reference tool (whether print, electronic, online, or CD-ROM) to locate the monographic version if the library has purchased this version but not a subscription to the source journal.
- individual articles/chapters in any Haworth publication are also available through the Haworth Document Delivery Service (HDDS).

Internet Applications in Euromarketing

CONTENTS

ABOUT THE EDITOR

Lynn R. Kahle, PhD, holds the James H. Warsaw Professorship in Marketing and has been Department Chair in the Department of Marketing at the University of Oregon. He has been on the faculty there in the Lundquist College of Business since 1983. As Department Chair he was instrumental in founding the highly regarded James H. Warsaw Sports Marketing Center.

Dr. Kahle has held positions in several countries. He taught in the Psychology Department at the University of Nebraska, served as Distinguished Eichoff Lecturer at Technion University in Haifa, Israel (2000); was Sir Allen Sewell Distinguished Visiting Fellow in Marketing at Griffith University, Gold Coast, Australia (1997); Distinguished Visiting Research Professor of Marketing Economics at the Norges Handelshøyskole (Norwegian School of Economics & Business Administration, Bergen, 1989); and Assistant Professor in the Department of Psychology at the University of North Carolina at Chapel Hill (1980-83).

Dr. Kahle has more than 100 publications in books and research articles in journals, including the *Journal of Consumer Psychology*, *Journal of Personality and Social Psychology*, *Sport Marketing Quarterly*, *Journal of Consumer Research*, *Public Opinion Quarterly*, *Child Development*, and *Journal of Marketing*. His books include *Attitudes and Social Adaptation*, *Social Values and Social Change*, *Marketing Management* (with Don Tull), *Cross-National Consumer Psychographics* (The Haworth Press, Inc.), and *Values, Lifestyles, and Psychographics* (with Larry Chiagouris). He has also served as Editor of *Sport Marketing Quarterly*.

Dr. Kahle is a Fellow in the American Psychological Association and the American Psychological Society, and a Fellow and Past-President of the Society for Consumer Psychology. Who's Who in the World and Who's Who Worldwide have included his biography.

Foreword

Professor Lynn R. Kahle is to be congratulated for editing this volume on Internet marketing. Scholars from Europe and the USA examine various facets of Internet usage both as a means of promotion and facilitator of purchasing and consumption decisions. This is one of the very first attempts looking at Internet marketing from cross-cultural and cross-national perspectives.

The results of the first study by Dijkstra and van Raaij confirm that research on media effects needs to take into account consumer product involvement. Consumer product involvement seems to be a crucial factor for the different effects of retrieval (print and Internet) and delivery (television) media. Retrieval media will be effective under conditions of high rather than low product involvement, because retrieval media have limited opportunity to involve and activate low-involved and passive consumers. Contrary to retrieval media, delivery media are better suited for influencing low-involved consumers. Delivery media may attract the attention of uninvolved consumers and, as a consequence, may induce superficial processing and low-involvement learning.

The results of this research may be useful for advertisers and media planners. It is worthwhile to know whether the same or similar advertising effects can be reached using less-expensive media or combinations of media. It is also useful to know for which products, brands, messages or target groups TV or multimedia are superior over print media and the Internet to reach communication and marketing objectives. After a number of similar studies on the effects of media (combinations), guidelines may be developed for media planning, not only based on reach and contact frequency, but also on the fit of media to the product,

---

[Haworth co-indexing entry note]: "Foreword." Kaynak, Erdener. Co-published simultaneously in *Journal of Euromarketing* (International Business Press, an imprint of The Haworth Press, Inc.) Vol. 11, No. 2, 2001, pp. xxi-xxiv; and: *Internet Applications in Euromarketing* (ed: Lynn R. Kahle) International Business Press, an imprint of The Haworth Press, Inc., 2001, pp. xiii-xvi. Single or multiple copies of this article are available for a fee from The Haworth Document Delivery Service [1-800-HAWORTH, 9:00 a.m. - 5:00 p.m. (EST). E-mail address: getinfo@haworthpressinc.com].

xiii

brand, message, and the knowledge and involvement of the target groups of consumers.

The synergy effects of combinations of media may contribute to creative insights in how media can be used in advertising campaigns, simultaneously and sequentially, to evoke the desired cognitive and affective responses to the message (brand) and consequently favorable attitudes and purchase intentions. The brand-related synergy seems to occur especially with low-involved consumers.

Internet advertising research has focused mostly on banner size, banner placement and media planning factors. In this paper, we explore the effects of price information and promotion in banner ads on the click-through rate (CTR), which is envisioned as a measure of product interest and potential purchase behavior. More specifically, is it useful to mention a price, a rebate or a gift to move the Internet user from the host site where the banner appears to the brand's web site?

The study by Chtourou et al. of a database including about 1200 ad insertions shows a major effect for banner looking like message from operating system. The industry sector, the size of the banner and its type of placement (targeted versus non-targeted) have significant impact on the click-through rate.

In addition, the study reveals that neither price nor promotional information has a direct effect on click-through rate. But interactions between mention of price of promotion and type of placement are significant. When the ads are targeted and when involved visitors are aware of the prices, mentioning price or promotion does not enhance the click-through rate. On the other hand mentioning promotion on non-targeted environments such as a home page may attract visitors and make them click on the banner.

When people already aware of the prices visit specific and targeted environments, they are less sensitive to prices, price rebates or promotion. This is especially true when prices included on the banners are incredibly low. Discovering the price of an item is probably one of the visitor's motivations, thus providing price directly on the banner may decrease this motivation to visit the web site and thus decrease the click-through rate. Three questions need further researchers: effect of monetary versus non-monetary promotion, effect of price mentioning in a specific shopping environment, importance of credibility when mentioning prices.

The paper by Kiecker and Cowles examines word-of-mouth (WOM) communication-one of the most powerful categories of personal influence in the marketplace-on the Internet. The power of WOM to motivate consumer attitudes and behaviors is well accepted in both academic and practitioner realms. While people generally think about WOM in terms of advice given and received within the context of face-to-face conversations, WOM communication can be transmitted in a variety of ways including in person, over the phone, through the mail and, with increasing frequency, via the Internet. Although the important role of WOM in the marketing communications mix is well-established, the study reported here is the first to examine the phenomenon *on the Internet*, where interpersonal communication processes can be viewed as among the most powerful influence mechanisms in our society today.

The paper begins with a brief summary of traditional WOM communication, especially its role as a subset of *personal influence*. We identify five traditional sources of interpersonal influence and describe the role that source *credibility* plays in the acceptance and use of WOM. We then offer a new typology for understanding WOM on the Internet, describing four distinct categories of online WOM. These two frameworks are used to discuss findings from a review of current online activities of consumers and businesses, providing examples of the different types of online WOM as exercised by different sources, exploring different credibility characteristics.

While marketers previously viewed personal influence as something that occurs when strong social ties exist between information receivers and senders (Brown and Reignen, 1987), such is not the case for online WOM. Due to the Internet, interpersonal communication is no longer restricted to the small circle of family and friends that personal sources were assumed to have, wherein source credibility was quite obvious and rarely suspect. It is our contention, therefore, that establishing credibility is essential in a setting such as the Internet, where business success increasingly will be determined by the extent to which consumers can trust the individuals and companies with which they interact. A better understanding of the determinants of source credibility in online interpersonal settings is needed to guide marketing strategies and tactics for the new media into the future. The background and initial framework for investigating online WOM developed here should serve as a foundation for future examinations of the specific nature of interpersonal communication and personal influence of the Internet.

According to Boush and Kahle, online discussions may be useful to marketing practitioners and academics for generating hypotheses and for providing thick description. Online discussions have some advantages over other sources of qualitative data. Postings leave a trace and can be archived for study. Unlike focus groups, online discussions are initiated by consumers themselves; however, as with focus groups, online discussions have the potential to lead managers in the wrong direction if vivid descriptions are substituted for thoughtful examination of the signals or for quantitative analysis. A more quantitative approach is possible using content analysis software.

Content analysis of online discussions differs from other application domains primarily because of the context supplied by the online community, especially the way the discussion is managed. Some online discussions differ from other application domains primarily because of the context supplied by the online community, especially the way the discussion is managed. Some online discussions are unmanaged and open to all while others restrict participation and monitor content. Online bulletin boards are also characterized by the nature of participants and their motivations. Messages in the discussion itself can be analyzed for both thematic and relational content. Marketers can improve the quality of discussion data by creating online panels whose members have known characteristics. Commercial web sites might accomplish this goal by encouraging membership in particular discussions. Similarly, research firms can create intranets with expert participants or scientific samples.

For managers considering changing their policies based on such content analysis, signal detection theory may aid in decision-making. Signal detection theory can provide a mechanism to help determine what is in fact true signal, based on the consequences of failing to detect a true signal or of mistaking noise for a true signal.

Erdener Kaynak

Media Effects by Involvement Under Voluntary Exposure: A Comparison of Television, Print and Static Internet

Majorie Dijkstra
W. Fred van Raaij

SUMMARY. In this study, the effects on consumer responses are explored of single-medium and multiple-media campaigns under two levels of consumer's product involvement. The results of this study confirm that research on media effects need to take into account consumer product involvement. Consumer involvement seems to be crucial for the differential effects of retrieval (print and Internet) and delivery (television) media. Retrieval media will be effective under conditions of high rather than low product involvement, because retrieval media have a limited capacity to influence low-involved and passive consumers. Delivery media are better suited for influencing low-involved consumers. Delivery media are able to attract the attention of low-involved consumers and, as a consequence, may induce superficial processing and low involvement learning. *[Article copies available for a fee from The Haworth Document Delivery Service: 1-800-HAWORTH. E-mail address: <getinfo@haworthpressinc.*

Majorie Dijkstra (E-mail: M.Dijkstra@kub.nl) is a PhD Student and W. Fred van Raaij (E-mail: W.F.vanraaij@kub.nl) is Full Professor of Economic Psychology, Department of Psychology, Tilburg University, P.O. Box 90153, 5000 LE, Tilburg, The Netherlands.

[Haworth co-indexing entry note]: "Media Effects by Involvement Under Voluntary Exposure: A Comparison of Television, Print and Static Internet." Dijkstra, Majorie, and W. Fred van Raaij. Co-published simultaneously in *Journal of Euromarketing* (International Business Press, an imprint of The Haworth Press, Inc.) Vol. 11, No. 2, 2001, pp. 1-21; and: *Internet Applications in Euromarketing* (ed: Lynn R. Kahle) International Business Press, an imprint of The Haworth Press, Inc., 2001, pp. 1-21. Single or multiple copies of this article are available for a fee from The Haworth Document Delivery Service [1-800-HAWORTH, 9:00 a.m. - 5:00 p.m. (EST). E-mail address: getinfo@haworthpressinc.com].

KEYWORDS. Media, Internet, advertising, experiment, involvement

INTRODUCTION

The emergence of 'new,' interactive media puts the control over the media increasingly in the hands of the consumer. New media such as the Internet enable active, selective exposure to information and interactivity, thus giving consumers the discretion to attend to particular information within a medium. Nowadays, it is the consumer who is doing the selection among *and* within media (Stewart, 1992). The nature of the interaction with media will increasingly determine the efficiency and effectiveness of media as communication tools (Stewart and Ward, 1994). As a consequence of these developments we expect that consumer involvement is an important factor for the effectiveness of media, because it influences whether or not consumers attend to a particular medium and a message within a medium. Research shows that consumer characteristics, such as involvement, directly influence media effects (Buchholz and Smith, 1991; Greenwald and Leavitt, 1984; Krugman, 1965). The involvement construct forms the basis of direct comparison of media effects. Research findings show that media differ in the extent to which they invite different kinds of attention and information processing of advertising (Stewart and Ward, 1994). In our previous experiments, we found strong product involvement effects, in some cases even overruling weaker media effects (Dijkstra, Buijtels, and Van Raaij, 2000, 2001). This indicates that the effectiveness of media varies with the level of consumer product involvement.

In this paper, we examine whether consumer product involvement determines the relative effectiveness of media. We examine the unique and joint effects of television, print and static Internet for low and high levels of consumer product involvement. The data set has been split at the median value of consumer product involvement to separate low- and high-involved consumers. We discuss the literature and develop hypotheses to be tested in an experimental study. Furthermore, we discuss the implications of this study for media planning and marketing-communication management.

MEDIA COMPARISONS AND EFFECTS

Media can be compared on many dimensions and, according to Stewart (1992), the number of dimensions is growing. Within the current media environment, however, it is important to consider three media characteristics, i.e., the number and nature of modalities of the medium, the control over the medium, and the interaction with different media.

The number and nature of modalities of the medium are often used as a dimension for media comparison (Edell, 1988; Edell and Keller, 1989; Jacoby, Hoyer and Zimmer, 1983; Kisielius and Sternthal, 1984). This refers to the mode of presentation (i.e., text, audio, picture or video) corresponding to the human senses used for processing the presented material. The common-sense notion is that the larger the number of sensory modes engaged in the communication process, the greater the likelihood of effective communication. Multiple sensory modes facilitate learning, because recognizing the meaning of information in one mode may facilitate the interpretation of meaning in another mode (Jacoby, Hoyer and Zimmer, 1983; Kisielius and Sternthal, 1984). According to this view, and also found in a previous study, television is superior to print and static Internet on memory and cognitive responses (Dijkstra, Buijtels and Van Raaij, 2000, 2001).

Control over the speed and sequence of information transfer is one of the most discriminating media factors. The medium may be controlled by the sender (*external pacing*) or by the receiver (*internal pacing*) (Pieters and Van Raaij, 1992). As a consequence of pacing, *delivery* and *retrieval media* may be distinguished (Van Raaij, 1998). Television is an example of a delivery medium with external pacing. Advertisers control the speed of information transfer and the order of information items in TV ads. Because of its transient character, TV does not facilitate consumers to process the presented information at their own pace. However, television, as a delivery medium using multiple sensory modes, may have cognitive impact even on low-involved consumers (Buchholz and Smith, 1991). Under low-involvement conditions consumers may engage in superficial processing and may produce cognitive responses, consistent with Krugman's (1965) 'low-involvement learning' hypothesis.

In contrast to television, print media and the Internet allow consumers to process the information at their own pace (internal pacing) and sequence. In addition, these retrieval media enable consumers to retain the information. This enhances the opportunity to process the information, facilitating cognitive processing (Jacoby, Hoyer and Zimmer,

1983). It is expected that print media and the Internet enhance cognitive responses, only if consumer involvement is sufficiently high. The nature of print media and the Internet requires more active and involved participants, because the processing of information of these media is a relatively demanding task (Krugman, 1965) and more under personal control. According to the "information-processing-parsimony hypothesis" (Holbrook, 1978), consumers attempt to minimize demanding cognitive endeavors, and would be unlikely to read information of little interest of them (Buchholz and Smith, 1991). These retrieval media also have limited opportunity to influence less involved or passive consumers (Buchholz and Smith, 1991). Low-involved consumers can easily skip the ads and read only information that is interesting to them. On the other hand, with high involvement, more elaborate information processing may occur.

Message involvement is higher for consumers that are interested in the product or in other elements of the message, e.g., the origin of the product. Laurent and Kapferer (1985) distinguish several antecedents of involvement: perceived product importance, subjective probability and perceived importance of the negative consequences of a bad buy, hedonic value and perceived sign value of the product class. The product in this study, a South-African wine, may be important and has hedonic and sign value for a number of consumers. These consumers may be involved with the message about this product.

Consumer level of involvement with the ad, brand or product category is expected to influence both the amount and type of cognitive responses. Celsi and Olson (1988) found that involvement influences the amount and direction of attention, focus of attention and comprehension processes, and the depth and breadth of elaboration during comprehension. Buchholz and Smith (1991) maintained that, in terms of the amount of cognitive responses, involved consumers engage in more effortful information-search and processing regardless of the type of medium. Moreover, involved consumers may elicit more thoughts directly related to the message (brand processing), whereas less involved consumers elicit more thoughts related to non-message cues such as the execution of the ad and source expertise (Laczniak, Muehling, and Grossbart, 1989; Steward and Ward, 1994). We thus expect that high-involved consumers will report more cognitive responses, have higher scores on brand claim recall, and may have a stronger positive or negative attitude toward the brand or the ad. Table 1 gives a summary of the media characteristics and their communication effects. Print media and static Internet have identical characteristics. The dimensions of a

TABLE 1. Effects of Media Dimensions on Information Processing and Consumer Responses

Medium	Dimension	Involvement	Effect on information processing & consumer responses
Television	Two sensory modes		More information processing and consumer responses (Dijkstra, Buijtels and Van Raaij, 1999; Jacoby, Hoyer and Zimmer, 1983; Kiselius and Sternthal, 1984).
	External pacing		Low opportunity to process and rehearse information (Jacoby et al., 1983).
	Delivery medium	Low/high	Passive information processing possible and low involvement learning (Krugman, 1965; Buchholz and Smith, 1991).
Print	One sensory mode		Less information processing and consumer responses (Dijkstra et al., 1999; Jacoby et al., 1983; Kiselius and Sternthal, 1984).
	Internal pacing		High opportunity to process and rehearse information (Jacoby et al., 1983).
	Retrieval medium	Low	Less information processing due to low involvement (Krugman, 1965; Buchholz and Smith, 1991).
		High	More information processing due to high involvement (Krugman, 1965; Buchholz and Smith, 1991)
Static Internet	One sensory mode		Less information processing and consumer responses (Dijkstra et al., 1999; Jacoby et al., 1983; Kiselius and Sternthal, 1984).
	Internal pacing		High opportunity to process and rehearse information (Jacoby et al., 1983).
	Retrieval medium	Low	Less information processing due to low involvement (Krugman, 1965; Buchholz and Smith, 1991).
		High	More information processing due to high involvement (Krugman, 1965; Buchholz and Smith, 1991).

medium contribute to the ability of a medium to communicate a message. The size of the contribution of each dimension to the communication power of the medium is an empirical question.

HYPOTHESES

Based on the literature on media characteristics and consumer product involvement, we state the following hypotheses:

H1: *Low-involved consumers exposed to static Internet or to print media will have similar cognitive and affective responses and similar brand claim recall.*

H2: *High-involved consumers exposed to static Internet or to print media will have similar cognitive and affective responses and similar brand claim recall.*

The communication effectiveness of static Internet and print media is expected to be largely similar, considering the senses stimulated and the speed and control of information transfer. However, the Internet and print media may differ in their communication effectiveness, because the delivery mechanism of these media differs. Sundar, Narayan, Obregon and Uppal (1998) stated that the paper on which the ad is printed allows for the readers' eyes to consume the page in its entirety, while the advertisement page on the computer has to be scrolled through to be processed. This may lead to cognitive differences between the Internet and print.

As discussed before, print media and the Internet require more involved consumers. As these media have limited opportunity to influence low-involved consumers, we might expect these media to be more effective for high-involved consumers, and to be as effective as TV. Because the level of involvement determines to a certain extent the effectiveness of print and Internet, and because television, as a delivery medium has cognitive impact even on low-involved consumers (Krugman, 1965; Buchholz and Smith, 1991), we state the following hypotheses:

H3: *Low-involved consumers exposed to television, as compared with low-involved consumers exposed to print media or to static Internet, will have more cognitive and affective responses, and higher brand claim recall.*

H4: *High-involved consumers exposed to only one medium, television, print or static Internet, will have similar cognitive and affective responses and similar brand claim recall, irrespective of the medium.*

MULTIPLE MEDIA VERSUS ONE MEDIUM

Based on the idea that each medium has unique capabilities and effects (Wright, 1980), synergy is expected if the same advertising message is communicated by multiple media. Synergy occurs when different media with their specific strengths complement each other in a campaign, or when the strength of one medium compensates for the weakness of the other medium.

For low-involved consumers, we expect that multiple-media campaigns are more effective than single-media campaigns, except for the TV-only campaign. In a multiple-media campaign, TV may attract attention to the advertisement and thus have cognitive impact on the low-involved consumer. After the TV ad created positive attitudes, low-involved consumers may also pay attention to the advertisements on the Internet and in the print media. However, we do not expect that low-involved consumers process the information in the print and/or Internet ad profoundly. In TV-only campaigns, there are three opportunities for so-called 'low-involvement learning' (Krugman, 1965). Therefore, we expect that TV-only campaigns are as effective as multiple-media campaigns in communicating an advertisement message.

Conversely, for high-involved consumers, we expect that multiple-media campaigns are more effective than TV-only campaigns. Again, TV may attract attention and may create interest for the print and Internet advertisements. Since the consumers are already more involved in the product and message, and these media allow the consumers to process the information at their own pace, we may expect more profound information processing of the Internet and print advertisement. We, therefore, state the following hypotheses:

H5: *Low-involved consumers exposed to the same advertisement in three media (print, Internet and TV) will have more cognitive and affective responses, and higher brand claim recall than low-involved consumers exposed three times to the same advertisement on the Internet or in print media.*

H6: *Low-involved consumers exposed to the same advertisement in three media (print, Internet and TV) will have similar cognitive and affective responses, and similar brand claim recall as low-involved consumers exposed three times to the same advertisement on television.*

H7: *High-involved consumers exposed to the same advertisement in three media (print, Internet and TV) will have more cognitive and affective responses, and higher brand claim recall than high-involved consumers exposed three times to the same advertisement in the same medium.*

RESEARCH METHODOLOGY

An experimental approach was used to study the effects of advertising in various media. One hundred and sixty-one consumers from the database of the Product Evaluation Laboratory of the Technical University of Delft participated. Eleven subjects are excluded from the analysis because they were aware of the objectives of the research. Subjects' ages ranged from 19 through 64 years (average age was 41 years), of which 71 were male and 79 female. As a reward for their participation, subjects received s/b: €10.

In this study, an incomplete design was used including only the effects of one and three media exposures. We tested three single-medium conditions (TV-only, print-only and Internet-only) and a multiple-media condition, consisting of television, print and static Internet. Although a laboratory setting is normally used in order to control exposure to stimuli, we allowed voluntary exposure to advertisements in order to be able to obtain insights in the *true* differences between media. We attempted to approximate reality and to increase external validity using replicas of living rooms, no time constraints, focusing subject's attention on news information, and giving respondents the opportunity to zap during exposure to the broadcast. Replicas of living rooms were used in order to make respondents feel more comfortable and less conscious of being part of an experiment. In addition, respondents in the TV-only and the multimedia condition were told they could watch two channels and they were equipped with a remote control device that allowed them to switch between channels. When the respondents turned on the TV and switched to channel 2, they 'fell' in the middle of the program. In this way, the volatility of the medium was maintained.

During the experiment the respondents were observed with cameras. The numbers of exposures to the target ad, the time spent on a medium, media use (sequential or simultaneous media usage) and the media sequences are observed. Dependent on the condition, respondents were told to read, to surf, and/or to watch news information. After exposure to the news items, subjects were asked to fill out a questionnaire to assess their responses to the ads (Table 2).

STIMULI

Communication stimuli for unfamiliar brands were developed in cooperation with an advertising agency. Using unfamiliar brands eliminates the differences between the subjects due to prior knowledge or attitudes associated with existing brands and ads (Edell and Keller, 1998).

TABLE 2. Explanation of the Media Conditions

Media condition	N	Exposure to communication stimuli
Television-only (TV-TV-TV)	31	Possibility to watch three 10-minute news programs. After each program followed an ad break that consisted of four 30-second ads: the target ad and the three filler ads. Subjects could zap to another channel.
Print-only (P-P-P)	37	Possibility to read three news magazines. Each magazine contained eight news pages and four full-page ads in full color: the target ad and the three filler ads.
Internet-only (I-I-I)	33	Possibility to surf on three news websites. Each website consisted of five scrolling news pages. On each news page, banner ads served as a link to the ad pages: the target ad page and three filler ad pages.
Multiple media (TV-P-I)	49	Possibility to watch one news program followed by one commercial break, to read one news magazine with the four ads, and to surf on one news website with links to the four ad pages.

The target ad was for a brand of wine. The wine commercial consisted of a picture of the wine bottle and its label (Oude Kaap, a South-African wine), pictures of vineyards, the Internet address, voice-over giving information about the wine, and background music. The print and the Internet ad were consistent with the TV ad in the amount of information given about the brand. The spoken words in the TV ad were used as written copy in the print and Internet ad. The Internet ad consisted of three pages: one page based on the print ad, one page with additional information about wine in general, and a page with a recipe for a meal. Most advertising web pages of Dutch companies are still static of form and do not yet include dynamic elements such as audio and movement. Therefore, we used static Internet without audio and dynamic visuals. The three filler ads (for an unfamiliar brand of rice, an audio-visual company, and a brand of tacos) were unrelated to the target ads. All ads were pre-tested on likability.

Three news broadcasts from a local news station were recorded and edited. Based on the informational content of the news broadcasts, the news magazine and news website were constructed. The news website was in an Intranet environment and consisted of news pages and advertising pages. Banners ads, consisting of a picture from the ad and the brand name served as link to the target ad and filler ad pages. A log file was used to trace how subjects moved through the website and how long they stayed at a specific page.

DEPENDENT VARIABLES

We collected modified cognitive responses by asking the respondents to write down what they were thinking, *and*, in a separate question, what they were feeling during the exposure to the advertisements. Especially, in the multiple-media condition, this question demands much capacity of the respondents, because they were asked to report on three advertising exposures. Therefore, we showed them a small, not readable extract from the advertisement that was framed (i.e., TV frame, a page frame or a computer screen frame) to prompt the respondent's memory.

Two graduate students coded the thoughts and feelings listing. A third person solved all disagreements. The thoughts were coded on two aspects, i.e., whether the thoughts were product or ad related and whether the thoughts were positive, negative or neutral. The feelings were coded whether they were product or ad related. Cohen's kappa, the measure of agreement between the coders, was for thoughts on average .78, and for feelings .72.

Subjects were asked to write down everything they remembered about the advertised brand to assess the number of brand claims correctly recalled. Cohen's kappa was .89.

Brand attitude benefit belief was constructed by weighting the subject's belief that the brand had certain attributes (7-point scale 'not at all likely'–'very likely') by the subject's evaluation of these attributes (from 'very bad' (-3) to 'very good' ($+3$)). Subjects indicated their overall brand liking on a 7-point scale from 'very favorable' to 'very unfavorable.'

All subjects were asked for their intention to buy and to order the advertised product in a restaurant. They indicated their intention on a 7-point scale (from 'extremely unlikely' to 'extremely likely').

Covariates affecting ad response were also measured. These covariates were subject's age, gender, prior product knowledge, product involvement (Edell and Keller, 1989) and general attitude toward advertising. Subjects with prior knowledge of the product category may have more positive attitudes. Likewise, attitude toward the medium may influence consumer judgments of the ad or the brand. Product involvement may influence the processing intensity and may lead to stronger positive or negative attitudes. The two facets of consumer product involvement, perceived product importance and interest (McQuarrie and Munson, 1992) were measured with two 7-point scales ('very unimportant' to 'very important' and 'very uninterested' to 'very interested'). Subjects were asked to indicate their knowledge about the product category on a 7-point scale ('not at all knowledgeable' to 'very knowledgeable'). General attitude toward advertising within the medium was measured on five item scales by asking subjects how informative, enjoyable, annoying, obtrusive and entertaining they judge advertising in general.

The values of Cronbach alpha for the multiple-item scales indicate a good internal consistency: purchase intention α = .88; wine involvement α = .83; general attitude toward advertising in the medium α = .78.

ANALYSIS AND RESULTS

As discussed in the literature, print media and the Internet require more involved consumers. Because these media have limited opportunity to influence low-involved consumers, we might expect these media to be more effective for high-involved consumers, and for them become as effective as TV. The analysis of covariance shows that the covariate "product involvement" has a large effect on the dependent variables. The ANCOVA indicates significant consumer involvement effects for brand claim recall (F = 11.99, p < .001), purchase intention (F = 21.63, p < .001), overall brand liking (F = 4.05, p < .05), and brand attitude benefit beliefs (F = 47.13, p < .001). This may indicate that media effects differ with the level of consumer product involvement.

Based on the median value (median involvement = 5), a split has been made between low-involved and high-involved subjects. Table 3 presents the means and significance tests of the processing variables for the media conditions.

The total number of thoughts and the total number of evaluative thoughts are an indicator of the amount of processing (Edell and Keller, 1989). In the single-media conditions, low-involved subjects have more total, evaluative, and brand-evaluative thoughts than high-involved subjects. This is contrary to our expectations that high-involved consumers process information deeper and better than low-involved consumers, and thus have more thoughts. Note that this concerns product involvement. The higher scores of low-involved subjects on total and evaluative thoughts may consist of ad-related thoughts. It cannot be explained why low (product) involved subjects have higher scores on

TABLE 3. Means for the Processing Variables for Low- and High-Involved Subjects[1]

	Total thoughts		Evaluative thoughts		Brand evaluative thoughts		Ad evaluative thoughts	
Involvement	Low	High	Low	High	Low	High	Low	High
Internet	3.05ᵃ	2.79ᵃ	1.79ᵃ	1.79ᵃ	0.74ᵃ	0.43ᵃ	1.05ᵃᵇ	1.36ᵃᵇ
Print	2.70ᵃ	2.14ᵃ	1.91ᵃ	1.36ᵃ	1.04ᵃ	0.50ᵃ	0.87ᵃ	0.86ᵃ
TV	4.56ᵇ	2.85ᵃ	3.17ᵇ	2.00ᵃ	1.28ᵃ	0.54ᵃ	1.89ᶜ	1.46ᵃᵇ
Multiple media	3.57ᵃᵇ	4.64ᵇ	2.75ᵃᵇ	3.80ᵇ	1.13ᵃ	1.92ᵇ	1.63ᵇᶜ	1.88ᵇ

[1] Analysis of Variance is used because there were no linear relationships between the dependent variables and covariates.

brand-related thoughts. In multiple-media conditions, high-involved subjects have more total and evaluative thoughts. This is according to our expectations.

For low-involved consumers, the ANOVA indicates marginal significant media exposure effects for total thoughts ($F = 2.17$, $p < .10$) and total evaluative thoughts ($F = 2.40$, $p < .10$). There are no significant media exposure effects for the other measures. Low-involved subjects in the TV-only condition report significantly more total thoughts and more evaluative thoughts than the print-only and the Internet-only subjects. Consistent with H1, there are no significant differences between print-only and Internet-only subjects. Contrary to H5, subjects in the multimedia condition did not report significantly more thoughts than the print-only and the Internet-only subjects. For brand evaluative thoughts, no significant differences were found. However, subjects in television-only condition elicited significantly more ad evaluative thoughts than the print-only and the Internet-only subjects. Visual stimuli seem to enhance the consumer ability to process superficial aspects of the advertising. The visual cues provided in TV commercials may draw the attention of the subjects away from the brand and encourage ad-related thinking. As a consequence, the TV condition might elicit more ad-related than brand-related thoughts.

For high-involved subjects, the analysis of variance shows significant media exposure effects for total thoughts ($F = 3.97$, $p < .05$), for evaluative thoughts ($F = 5.17$, $p < .01$), and brand evaluative thoughts ($F = 4.72$, $p < .01$). The analysis indicates no significant media exposure effects for ad evaluative thoughts. High-involved subjects in the single medium conditions did not differ significantly between media conditions on the processing measures. This is consistent with H4. Consistent with H7, high-involved subjects in the multimedia condition elicited significantly more thoughts, more evaluative thoughts and more brand-related thoughts than the high-involved subjects in the TV-only, Internet-only and print-only conditions. Moreover, subjects in the multimedia condition report more ad-related thoughts than print-only subjects.

Table 4 presents the means and significance tests of the feeling measures. For low-involved subjects, the analysis of variance indicates no significant media-exposure effects. The results show no significant differences between media conditions for total feelings and brand feelings. Similar to the pattern found for ad-related thoughts, low-involved subjects exposed to TV or to multiple media elicit more ad-related feelings than subjects exposed to print.

For high-involved subjects, the ANOVA indicated a significant media effect for total feelings ($F = 6.42$, $p < .01$) and brand-related feelings ($F = 5.80$, $p < .01$), but not for ad-related feelings ($F = 1.73$, $p > .10$). Similar to results for the processing measures and consistent with H4, high-involved subjects in the single-medium conditions did not differ significantly between media on the feeling measures.

Consistent with H7, high-involved subjects in the multimedia condition reported significantly more feelings and more brand-related feelings than high-involved subjects in the single-medium conditions. Moreover, subjects in the multimedia condition report more ad-related feelings than print-only subjects.

Table 5 presents the means and significance tests of memory and evaluation measures for low-involved and high-involved subjects. For low-involved subjects, the analysis of variance of brand claim recall results into a significant media condition effect ($F = 4.07$, $p < .01$). Con-

TABLE 4. Means for the Feeling Measures of Low-Involved and High-Involved Subjects[1]

Involvement	Total feelings		Brand feelings		Ad feelings	
	Low	High	Low	High	Low	High
Internet	1.95[a]	1.50[a]	0.84[a]	0.43[a]	1.11[ab]	1.07[ab]
Print	1.87[a]	1.36[a]	1.09[a]	0.57[a]	0.78[a]	0.79[a]
TV	2.89[a]	1.69[a]	1.28[a]	0.31[a]	1.61[b]	1.38[ab]
Multiple media	2.67[a]	3.36[b]	1.17[a]	1.76[b]	1.50[b]	1.60[b]

[1] Analysis of Variance is used because there were no linear relationships between the dependent variables and covariates.

sistent with H3, low-involved subjects exposed to TV or to multiple media recall significantly more brand claims than subjects exposed to the Internet or print. Consistent with H1, there is no significant difference in the number correctly recalled brand claims between the Internet-only and print-only conditions. Neither do subjects in the TV condition recall more brand claims than subjects in the multiple-media condition.

For high-involved subjects, the analysis of variance of brand claim recall does not show a significant media effect. As a result, the findings indicate that there are no significant differences between the media conditions. Contrary to the expectations, subjects in the multiple-media condition did not recall more brand claims than the subjects in the single-medium conditions.

For the low-involved subjects, the analysis of covariance of purchase intention shows no significant media effect ($F = 1.72$, $p < .20$). On the other hand, we find a significant main effect of general attitude toward the advertising ($F = 9.99$, $p < .001$) and consumers involvement with wine ($F = 10.95$, $p < .0001$). Correcting for these covariates, the ANCOVA indicates that low-involved subjects in the Internet condition have significantly lower purchase intention than subjects in the TV and multimedia conditions. Even among only low-involved subjects, consumer involvement has an influence on purchase intention. It seems that purchase intention is predominantly determined by consumer attitude toward advertising and consumer product involvement, and to a lesser extent by the medium in which they saw the advertisement.

For high-involved subjects, no significant main effect has been found of general attitude toward the advertising and consumer product involvement. The ANOVA of purchase intention indicates a marginal significant media exposure effect ($F = 2.38$, $p < .10$). Subjects in the

TABLE 5. Means for Memory and Evaluation Measures for Low- and High-Involved Subjects

	Brand claims recall		Overall brand liking		Brand attitude benefit beliefs		Purchase intention	
Involvement	*Low*	*High*	*Low*	*High*	*Low[1]*	*High[1]*	*Low[1]*	*High*
Internet	1.74[a]	2.50[a]	4.33[ab]	4.46[a]	5.23[a]	8.55[a]	1.71[a]	2.13[a]
Print	1.83[a]	3.21[a]	3.96[a]	4.38[a]	6.03[a]	8.95[a]	2.19[ab]	3.14[b]
TV	2.89[b]	3.31[a]	4.78[b]	5.00[ab]	8.71[b]	10.92[ab]	2.47[b]	3.13[b]
Multiple media	3.25[b]	3.44[a]	4.46[ab]	5.12[b]	6.37[ab]	12.35[b]	2.46[b]	3.16[b]

[a,b] means with the same letter within a column do not differ significantly from one another (on 5%)
[1] means are corrected for wine involvement and general attitude toward advertising

Internet condition have a significantly lower purchase intention than subjects in the print, TV and multimedia conditions.

For low-involved subjects, the ANOVA of overall brand liking indicates no significant main effect of media exposure ($F = 1.59$, $p > .10$). However, subjects in the TV condition have significantly higher overall brand liking than subjects in the print condition. There is no significant difference between the TV, the Internet and multimedia conditions.

For the high-involved subjects, the ANOVA of brand liking gives a marginally significant media exposure effect ($F = 2.24$, $p < .10$). Subjects in the multimedia condition evaluate the brand higher than print-only and Internet-only subjects. The differences between the TV, print and Internet conditions are not significant.

For low-involved subjects, the analysis of covariance of brand attitude benefit beliefs indicates no significant media condition effect ($F = 1.88$, $p > .10$). In contrast, a significant main effect has been found for consumer product involvement ($F = 11.12$, $p < .001$). TV subjects have a more favorable brand attitude than subjects in the Internet and print conditions. Contrary to H5, using multiple media was not more effective in creating brand attitude benefit beliefs than using only one medium.

For high-involved subjects, the ANCOVA of brand attitude benefit beliefs gives a significant main effect of media ($F = 4.48$, $p < .01$) and consumer product involvement ($F = 5.38$, $p < .05$). As hypothesized, the single-medium conditions did not differ in brand attitude. Subjects in the multimedia condition have a more favorable brand attitude than print and Internet-only subjects.

DISCUSSION

The purpose of this study is to compare the effectiveness of media for low-involved and high-involved subjects. In this experiment, the external validity was increased by not forcing subjects to a certain use of media, but creating a more 'realistic' living-room environment and letting subjects free in their use of media.

Consistent with H1 and H2, we found no significant differences between the print-only and Internet-only conditions. Both for low-involved and high-involved consumers, static Internet is as effective as print in evoking cognitive and affective responses, and recalling brand claims. Also, for the attitude measures, we obtained no significant differences between these two media conditions. Only high-involved subjects in the Internet condition have a significant lower purchase intention than high-involved subjects in the print condition.

Consistent with H3, low-involved consumers in the TV-only condition report more cognitive responses and recalled significantly more brand claims than consumers in the print-only and the Internet-only conditions. Although the pattern is consistent with the hypothesis, the TV condition did not evoke significantly more feelings than the Internet condition. Moreover, low-involved TV-subjects had higher brand attitude beliefs than print and Internet subjects, and higher purchase intention than Internet subjects. The results show that, compared with print and the Internet, television is superior in evoking cognitive responses. This is consistent with the findings of Kisielius and Sternthal (1984) and the view that a larger number of sensory modes lead to more effective communication (Jacoby, Hoyer and Zimmer, 1983). Due to the combination of visual and audio modes, TV evokes more attention and has thus more impact than the Internet and print. As a consequence, low-involved subjects processed the television ads and Krugman's (1965) 'learning without involvement' may have occurred.

Consistent with H4, high-involved TV-subjects had similar cognitive and affective responses and brand claim recall as high-involved subjects in the print- and Internet-conditions. There was only a significant difference in purchase intention between TV-only and Internet-only subjects.

Contrary to H5, low-involved consumers in the multiple media condition did not report more thoughts and feelings than consumers in the print-only and Internet-only conditions. The findings also do not show higher brand liking or a more favorable brand attitude of the multiple-media consumers. Although multiple-media consumers recalled more brand claims and had a higher purchase intention than subjects in the print and Internet conditions, there may have been an interference effect. Low-involved consumers might find it difficult to integrate the messages of different media.

Consistent with H6, low-involved consumers in the multiple-media condition had similar cognitive and affective responses, and similar brand claim recall as low-involved consumers in the TV-only condition. Moreover, consumers in the TV-only and multiple-media conditions had the same attitude toward the brand and purchase intention.

Consistent with H7, high-involved consumers exposed to multiple-media reported more cognitive and affective responses than high-involved consumers exposed to a single medium. Contrary to H7, we did not find significant differences for brand claim recall between the single-medium and multiple-media conditions. Although the findings revealed that consumers in the multiple-media condition liked the brand more and had a more favorable attitude toward the brand than consumers in the Internet and print conditions. The multiple-media and TV-only conditions did not differ on the memory and evaluation measures.

The means and significance tests for the low-involved consumers confirm the idea that attention getting media, such as TV, are more effective in transmitting messages to low-involved consumers than internally paced media such as print and the Internet. These media require more active and involved consumers. Also, the combination of media is effective in creating brand claim recall among low-involved consumers. Moreover, the chance that the advertising message reaches the audience is larger when multiple media are used to communicate the message.

For high-involved consumers, media do not differ that much in generating brand claim recall, in creating purchase intention and brand attitudes. This indicates that for high-involved consumers, retrieval media may be as effective as delivery media.

The results diverge regarding the expected synergy effect of multiple-media conditions. For the message communicated by multiple media, high-involved consumers report more cognitive and affective responses, but do not recall more brand claims than high-involved consumers receiving the message through a single medium. The synergy effect may thus not be directed toward the brand, the content of the advertising messages.

As the number of thoughts is an indicator of the degree of information processing, we might expect that more thoughts lead to higher brand claim recall. Correlations show for the high-involved consumers no significant correlation between the total number of thoughts and the number of brand claims recalled $(.17, p > .10)$. A possible explanation is that high-involved consumers receiving the same ad through different media perceive the ads as new. Therefore, each exposure to the ad in a new medium draws their attention and will be processed, leading to more thoughts. The focus will be more on the ad (ad-related thoughts) because the ad is new, and in this way takes the attention away from the brand information, thus not leading to higher brand claim recall. Another explanation is that each medium elicits its own thoughts, leading to more thoughts altogether.

For low-involved consumers on the other hand, we found a significant correlation between the number of thoughts and brand claim recall $(.28, p < .01)$. Low-involved consumers seem to recall more if their level of information processing is higher. The expected synergy effect directed towards the brand, the content of the advertising messages, seems to be present for low-involved consumers.

IMPLICATIONS

The results of this study confirm that research on media effects needs to take into account consumer product involvement. Consumer product involvement seems to be crucial factor for the differential effects of retrieval (print and Internet) and delivery (television) media. Retrieval media will be effective under conditions of high rather than low product involvement, because retrieval media have limited opportunity to involve and activate low-involved and passive consumers. Contrary to retrieval media, delivery media are better suited for influencing low-involved consumers. Delivery media may attract the attention of low-involved consumers and, as a consequence, may induce superficial processing (Buchholz and Smith, 1991) and low-involvement learning (Krugman, 1965). Note that delivery media may also be effective under high-involvement conditions.

The results of this research are useful for advertisers and media planners. It is worthwhile to know whether the same or similar advertising effects can be reached using less expensive media or combinations of media. It is also useful to know for which products, brands, messages or target groups TV or multimedia are superior over print media and the Internet to reach communication and marketing objectives. After a number of similar studies on the effects of media (combinations), guidelines may be developed for media planning, not only based on reach and contact frequency, but also on the fit of media to the product, brand, message, and the knowledge and involvement of the target groups of consumers.

The synergy effects of combinations of media may contribute to creative insights in how media can be used in advertising campaigns, simultaneously and sequentially, to evoke the desired cognitive and affective responses to the message (brand) and consequently favorable attitudes and purchase intentions. The brand-related synergy seems to occur especially with low-involved consumers.

LIMITATIONS

The common limitations of laboratory studies investigating different media are the research setting and the short time interval between ad exposure and answering the questionnaire. These limitations also apply to this experiment. On the other hand, in an experiment there is more control over the experimental setting to study differences between conditions.

Our experiment was designed to measure media effects under voluntary exposure. This approach has as a limitation that the number of and duration of exposures to the ads cannot be held constant, as in controlled media experiments. Although we held the confrontation situation, that is the chance of being exposed to the advertisements constant, subjects' media behavior determines whether or not, how long and how often they are exposed to the advertisements.

Moreover, this experiment was not designed to examine media effects under different levels of involvement. Consumer product involvement was not manipulated but measured. But even without a manipulation of involvement, we obtained a strong involvement effect on the effectiveness of delivery and retrieval media.

The type of product, brand or message may influence the relative effectiveness of media. The product of this experiment was a brand of wine. The results of this experiment may be generalized to fast moving consumer goods, and not necessarily to consumer durables and services, and to business-to-business goods and services. Information about more complex and high-involving products or services may be better communicated through retrieval media that consumers can process at their own pace. Likewise, the message in this experiment was a relatively simple message on grapes, wine growing and a South African brand of wine. The results may not be generalized to complex messages. TV advertising is often unsuitable for complex messages, whereas print media and the Internet may be better suited for these messages. In a multimedia condition, according to the complementarity effect, TV may get the attention, whereas print media and the Internet may elaborate the message further.

We kept the informational content of the ads constant across media, and used similar visuals for the ads in different media. However, we are not able to make the ads completely similar due to the media characteristics (i.e., TV with audio and moving visuals). These differences in ad characteristics may have influenced the results of this study. However, in our view, these media characteristics and differences determine the communication power of each medium, and constitute the complementarity of media.

FUTURE RESEARCH DIRECTIONS

In this experiment, the effects of static Internet were examined. Increasingly, advertisers are using audio and moving visuals in their web pages. Future media research should examine the effectiveness of this dynamic form of the Internet. In this experiment, we found that static Internet and print have a similar effectiveness. It might be interesting to test whether the effects of dynamic Internet are similar to TV, except for the differences in external pacing.

Several studies examined the two-way interaction between TV, print and radio (Buchholz and Smith, 1991; Edell and Keller, 1989, 1998; Jacoby, Hoyer and Zimmer, 1983). The Internet provides a new way of communication with consumers. Examining two-way interactions between (static and dynamic) Internet and the traditional media will give more insights as to how the Internet might complement traditional media in multiple-media advertising campaigns.

The construct 'consumer product involvement' warrants further analysis. Manipulations may create artificial differences in involvement, or consumers may be selected with different levels of involvement. The antecedents of product involvement (importance, perceived risk, hedonic value) may, however, differ (Laurent and Kapferer, 1985), leading to different consequences for advertising and media usage.

REFERENCES

Buchholz, L.M., and Smith, R.E. (1991). The role of consumer involvement in determining cognitive response to broadcast advertising. *Journal of Advertising*, 20, 4-17.

Celsi, R.L., and Olson, J.C. (1988). The role of involvement in attention and comprehension processes. *Journal of Consumer Research*, 15, 210-225.

Dijkstra, M., Buijtels, H.E.J.M, and Van Raaij, W.F. (2001). The separate and joint effects of medium type on consumer responses: A comparison of television, print and the Internet. *Journal of Business Research*, forthcoming.

Dijkstra, M., Buijtels, H.E.J.M, and Van Raaij, W.F. (2000). The separate and joint effects of medium type on consumer responses under voluntary exposure: A comparison of television, print and static Internet. In D.R. Deeter-Schmelz, and T.P. Hartman, (Eds.), *Marketing Advances in the New Millennium* (pp. 286-291). Athens: Society of Marketing Advances.

Edell, J.A. (1988). Nonverbal effects in ads: A review and synthesis. In S. Hecker and D.W. Stewart (Eds.), *Nonverbal Communication in Advertising* (pp. 11-27). New York: Lexington Books.

Edell, J.A., and Keller, K.L. (1989). The information processing of coordinated media campaigns. *Journal of Marketing Research*, 26, 149-163.

Edell, J.A., and Keller, K.L. (1998). Analyzing media interactions: Print reinforcement of television ad campaigns. *Working paper*. Durham, NC: Fuqua School of Business, Duke University.

Greenwald, A.G., and Leavitt, C. (1984). Audience Involvement in advertising: Four levels. *Journal of Consumer Research*, 11, 581-592.

Holbrook, M.B. (1978). Beyond attitude structure. *Journal of Marketing Research*, 15, 546-556.

Jacoby, J., Hoyer, W.D., and Zimmer, M.R. (1983). To read, view, or listen? A cross-media comparison of comprehension. *Current Issues and Research in Advertising*. Ann Arbor: University of Michigan, 201-217.

Kisielius, J., and Sternthal, B. (1984). Detecting and explaining vividness effects in attitudinal judgments. *Journal of Marketing Research*, 21, 54-64.

Krugman, H.E. (1965). The impact of television advertising: Learning without involvement. *Public Opinion Quarterly*, 29, 349-356.

Laurent, G., and Kapferer, J.-N. (1985). Measuring consumer involvement profiles. *Journal of Marketing Research*, 22, 41-53.

Laczniak, R.N., Muehling, D.D., and Grossbart, S. (1989). Manipulating message involvement in advertising research. *Journal of Advertising*, 18, 28-38.

McQuarrie, E.F., and Munson, J.M. (1992). Product involvement inventory: Improved usability and validity. *Advances in Consumer Research*, 19, 108-115.

Pieters, R.G.M., and Van Raaij, W.F. (1992). *Reclamewerking [How Advertising Works]*. Houten: Stenfert Kroese.

Stewart, D.W. (1992). Speculations on the future of advertising research. *Journal of Advertising*, 21, 1-18.

Stewart, D.W., and Ward, S. (1994). Media effects on advertising. In J. Bryant and D. Zillmann (Eds.), *Media Effects: Advances in Theory and Research* (pp. 315-363). Hillsdale NJ: Lawrence Erlbaum Associates.

Sundar, S.S., Narayan, S., Obregon, R., and Uppal, C. (1998). Does web advertising work? Memory for print versus online media. *Journalism and Mass Communication Quarterly*, 75, 822-835.

Triesman, A.M. (1964). Verbal cues, language and meaning in selective attention. *American Journal of Psychology*, 77, 206-219.

Van Raaij, W.F. (1998). Interactive communication: Consumer power and initiative. *Journal of Marketing Communications*, 4, 1-8.

Wright, P.L. (1980). Message-evoked thoughts: Persuasion research using thought verbalizations. *Journal of Consumer Research*, 7, 151-75.

Effect of Price Information and Promotion on Click-Through Rates for Internet Banners

Mohamed Saber Chtourou
Jean Louis Chandon
Monique Zollinger

SUMMARY. The area of Internet advertising research has, up to now, focused mostly on banner size, placement and media planning factors. The purpose of this paper is to explore the effects of price information and promotion in banner ads on the click-through rate (CTR), which can be a predictor of product interest and potential purchase behavior. The study of a database including about 1200 ad insertions reveals that neither price nor promotional information has a direct effect on CTR. But interactions between mention of price or promotion and type of placement are significant. *[Article copies available for a fee from The Haworth Document Delivery Service: 1-800-HAWORTH. E-mail address: <getinfo@ haworthpressinc.com> Website: <http://www.HaworthPress.com> © 2001 by The Haworth Press, Inc. All rights reserved.]*

KEYWORDS. Internet, advertising banner, price, promotion, information processing, perception, reference price

Mohamed Saber Chtourou and Jean Louis Chandon are affiliated with CEROG IAE Aix en Provence. Monique Zollinger is affiliated with CERMAT, IAE de Tours.

Address correspondence to: Dr. Jean Louis Chandon, IAE Aix en Provence. BP 33 Clos Guiot 13540 Puyricard (E-mail: chandon@univ-aix.fr).

The authors wish to thank Wanadoo Régie for supporting this research.

[Haworth co-indexing entry note]: "Effect of Price Information and Promotion on Click-Through Rates for Internet Banners." Chtourou, Mohamed Saber, Jean Louis Chandon, and Monique Zollinger. Co-published simultaneously in *Journal of Euromarketing* (International Business Press, an imprint of The Haworth Press, Inc.) Vol. 11, No. 2, 2001, pp. 23-40; and: *Internet Applications in Euromarketing* (ed: Lynn R. Kahle) International Business Press, an imprint of The Haworth Press, Inc., 2001, pp. 23-40. Single or multiple copies of this article are available for a fee from The Haworth Document Delivery Service [1-800-HAWORTH, 9:00 a.m. - 5:00 p.m. (EST). E-mail address: getinfo@haworthpressinc.com].

Most of the time, information about price is used in retail-oriented promotions, its role being either to attract customers to a store or to convince people already in the store to buy the promoted item. Considering the ad for a price promotion on a web site, in the same way, we can distinguish two cases: either the promoted price is advertised on a banner outside the website offering the product, or, on the website itself. Whatever the medium is, the information about price promotion has the same objective and/or limits. If outside the point of purchase or website, the information may be useless for the customer who is not concerned with a specific deal for this product, thus ignoring the offer unless he/she shows a strong involvement with the product and wants (and or has the time) to perform ongoing research about the product offer (Engel, Blackwell, Miniard, 1995). If the information is advertised within the point-of-purchase, its expected effects are directly related to product purchases.

A recent study among managers (*Incentive Magazine*, 2000) about the effect of messages delivered with a gift reveals that the Internet is frequently used but not as successfully as conventional media. Amongst the media used for consumer promotion, the Internet ranks third with 46% of responses, just behind direct mail (67%), point-of-purchase (53%) and ahead of magazines (39%), newspapers (33%), packaging, radio, samplings and television. According to the managers sampled in this article, only 22% of them rank Internet as "extremely effective" against 63% for conventional media.

Consequently, several research questions arise about the reasons why Internet promotions may be less effective: would the difference between Internet users and non-users not be the only explanation? Or would the major differences in market structures and transparency affect the efficiency of promotion? Our objective is more modest. We are interested only in the effect of the mention of price, gift or rebate on banner ad effectiveness measured by the click-through rate. A recent study (Degeratu, Rangaswamy and Wu, 2000) shows that, among other search attributes, price appears to be perceived differently online versus offline (traditional supermarkets): price sensitivity seems higher online, but the combined effect of price and promotion on choice is weaker online than offline. Many executives are concerned that online consumers will focus on price and this would result in strong price competition. But the analyses revealed more complex relationships between online consumers and price, even if people currently online become comparable to the general population and thus just as (little?) price sensitive (Degeratu, Rangaswamy and Wu, 2000). Here we do not study price sensitivity in terms of buying behavior. Instead, we are investigating information search behavior. Our research question is the following: Is it useful to mention a price, rebate or gift to move the Internet user from the host site where the banner appears to the brand web site? Our approach will be exploratory. Using analysis of variance on a large data base of 1134 banners, we will try to disentangle the effect of price information and promotion from the effect of banner format, banner placement and media planning factors.

THEORETICAL BACKGROUND

Historically, Internet advertising research has focused on banner format (Hussherr, 1999; Chtourou and Chandon, 2000) and media planning factors. The media factors most often studied are the type of page (Home page versus other pages) often referred as "page placement," repetition (Hoffmann, Novak and Chatterjee, 1998), and number of impressions. Briggs and Hollis (1997) point out three main individual factors: the natural tendency to click on banners, involvement towards the product category and a special interest in the brand or product. A major survey (Infoseek in Onnein-Bonnefoy, 1997) was carried out on 550 banners. Three main characteristics of the ad formulation: the text presented as a question, the indication "click here" and a reference to price information (free, promotion or attractive price) were studied. Only one of the three possible determinants appears to be relevant: the presence of "click here" was proved to increase the click-through rates by 44%.

To explore the question of the effect of price information in banners on click-through rates, first we have tried to define what a click really means, and then considered how price information or promotion might motivate a click on the banner.

What Does a Click-Through Mean?

Clicking on the banner has been described as an indicator of the interest of the Internet user in the claim of the commercial (Bourliataux in Hussherr, 1999). Pavlou and Stewart (2000) consider it as a measure of the breadth and depth of information search which can be a predictor of product interest and potential purchase behavior. In fact, it is a deliberate action which means that the Internet user accepts to leave the site he was browsing to get in the announcer's website either to collect extra information or to conclude a transaction. This aspect of the persuasion process is specific to the Internet; the clicker can be regarded as a potential buyer.

But the click-through rate is not the only measure of banner effectiveness (Briggs and Hollis, 1997, among others). Clicking is only one step in a whole persuasion process. Many authors proposed models of Internet advertising, which integrate the specifics of this new media (Bourliataux in Hussherr 1999, see Figure 1). The click expresses only an extremely short-term (within the same visit) effect since people can be interested in the claim but defer the visit until completion of their current browsing.

Therefore, we can consider that the click-through rate is particularly suited for our study since the aim of the promotion tactics (such as price mention, gift and rebate studied here) is mainly to have short term (within the same campaign) effect on sales (Chandon, 1994). The stage of information processing that brings a click after being exposed to a banner are described in Figure 1.

FIGURE 1. The Stages in Mental Information Processing of the Internet Ad

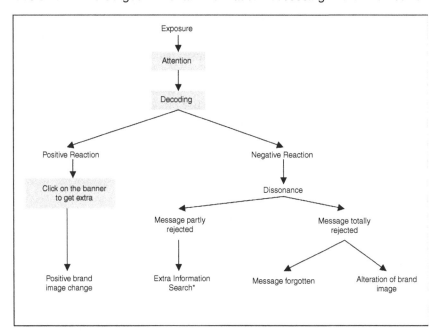

adapted from Bourliataux S., "Les raisons de l'efficacité publicitaire sur Internet" in Hussherr (1999), p. 85.

Price and Information Research

The information research on price requires a special involvement, a price sensitivity that is not only driven by budget limits. Within the same income limits, the level of price sensitivity may vary widely among consumers and increase with: difficulty to compare brands, the amount of expense on the product category and price knowledge. But the level of the customer's information on prices cannot be revealed only by memorization (Desmet and Zollinger, 1997; Monroe and Lee, 1999). This memorization globally seems rather weak, relatively unreliable and mainly stimulated by the frequency of product purchase. Hence, it appears that price knowledge is a less relevant variable than the degree of confidence of the consumer in the information has in mind in his implicit or explicit memory (Monroe and Lee, 1999).

For a customer, price is an information that is perceived, and then altered, according to references that allow to judge if a price is, subjectively, expensive or not. The prevailing view (Janiszewski and Lichtenstein, 1999) in the pricing literature is that subjective price judgments rely on a comparison of market prices to a standard price (Thaler, 1985; Monroe, 1990; Zollinger, 1993) according to Adaptation-level Theory (Helson, 1964).

When evaluating a product, the price level perception is influenced by: income, the consumption situation, brand image as well as expected quality and average price for this category of product. To find the required information to settle his judgment, the consumer will search in his memory, for prices paid or seen before (internal reference price, IRP) or in his environment (external reference price, ERP) through observation of the offers of one or several points-of-purchase. The IRP is founded on prior beliefs according to a former purchase (historical price) or on the estimation of a fair price (expected price). When the customer has no IRP, he relies on ERP. Retailers may then be tempted to use ERP to stimulate purchases via odd-even prices, reduced prices or even discount rates. This question is especially relevant when the consumer has to convert prices expressed in a foreign currency, which can be quite usual on the Web. However, price information on the banners may not be viewed as important because experienced Internet users can operate search agents to have automatic price comparisons. In other words, Internet users might feel confident in their ability to evaluate the attractiveness of the proposed price using a shopping robot (shopbot). It is also possible that internet users are less sensitive to price than offline buyers since they value more convenience and ease of buying, enquiring for product price is not as costly than it is in the differently "real world" (no shopping trip needed, delivery to the house, etc.).

Price and Inferences on Other Attributes

Price is not only considered as a monetary sacrifice (Murphy and Enis, 1986), but as a piece of information processed by the consumer to infer quality and value (Zeithaml, 1988; Rao and Monroe, 1989). This process is supported by an important theoretical background: Signaling theory (Simester, 1995) and inference theory (Alba and Hutchinson, 1987). It appears that price is used as a quality signal when product quality is difficult to appreciate from tangible cues. When assessing a positive relationship between price and manufacturing cost, the customer infers that a high price is related to good quality product. The effect is mostly revealed at the two ends on demand curve, where price elasticity has positive value: for cheapest items considered as insufficient quality products, and at the opposite for the highest-priced products.

When price is used as a numerical stimuli, we have to consider some of the principles of price perception (Monroe, 1990; Monroe and Lee, 1999):

1. Price perceptions are relative to other prices.
2. Consumers have a reference price for each discernible quality level for each product category and this price influences judgments of other prices.
3. There is a region of indifference about a reference price such that changes in price within this region produce no apparent change in perception.
4. The reference price may be some average of a range of prices for similar products and need not correspond to actual price.
5. Buyers do not judge each price singly; rather, each price is compared with the reference price and other prices in the price range.

These principles of price perception stress that judgments about prices are comparative, but the consumer may not discriminate between two prices, different but very close. It has been predicted that the emergence of the Internet as a communication channel would lead to an information explosion and result in lower prices and more competition amongst firms. We may wonder whether the increasing availability of comparative price information online affects the perception of price promotion when price is presented on a web page without any other reference price (ERP in that case).

RESEARCH QUESTIONS

Since the paper is mainly exploratory especially in the internet context we will address research questions rather than hypothesis.

When considering the reaction of consumers, measured by the click-through rate, when exposed to web information, price can be studied solely or comparatively. The price attribute can be regarded as one of many stimuli under the influence of moderating variables such as familiarity with the product, banner format and placement. In our study the research question can be formulated as *"Does price information: mentioning nominal price or using promotion techniques (gift, rebate or "free" mention) have a positive effect on the click-through rate?"*

The price information can be available on a banner under several forms: the price must be the main cue either as a price in absolute value or as a special promotion. The available data (see further down) does not allow us to test specifically each of the three different types of promotion since the sample size in each cell would be too small. The research question we set to explore can be formulated as follows:

Q1.   Does the use of promotion techniques in banners affect click-through rates (CTR)?

Q1.1. Does the mention of price in a banner affect click-through rates?

Q1.2. Does promotion (gift, rebate or mention "free") in banners affect click-through rates?

Some product categories are bought online more frequently than others. We speculate that an internal reference price is more likely for those categories (approached here by the announcers' sector). Unfortunately, we cannot test this interaction since sample size of the cells in the cross table were particularly small (see Appendix 1 for details). We explore the direct effect of sector since discussion with professionals suggested that the click-through rate should vary among sectors. We ask then a second research question:

Q2.   Does the product category affect click-through rate (CTR)?

Involvement

Many studies have shown the importance of involvement in the persuasion process. One can postulate, without too much risk, that Internet users who consult a targeted page will be more involved in the subject of this page than the average Internet user. Indeed, the dimension "interest" is one of the facets of involvement in most of the scales (Strazzieri, 1994). Internet users doing a thematic search or a keyword search should be more attentive to the advertisement, because of its affinity with their subject of interest. Those Internet users may be more inclined to seek additional information about the product. They should "click" more often than the less involved Internet users, like those exposed randomly to a banner displayed in "general rotation" or to a banner displayed in the Home page of the site. This supposition was generally validated either by professionals or academic studies (Hussher, 1999).

We postulate here that ads placed in thematic and Key word research result pages are better targeted than other placements and that they face customers who are more involved than others. So we can suppose that targeted placements (thematic and key word result pages) have a higher click-through rate than the other placements (general rotation and home page). Our third research question can be formulated as follows:

Q3.   Do banners in targeted placement have better CTR than banners in non targeted placement?

On the other hand, we can suggest that Involvement in the product category should affect the effect of price information. Involved customers should be more familiar with the product category. They are more likely to have internal reference price. Then presenting an external reference price (through price mentioning attractive prices or rebates) should decrease the credibility of the offer. We can then suppose that we will have an interaction between involvement (approached here by the type of the placement) and price mention or promotion.

Q4.   Is there an interaction between promotion techniques and the type of placement on the CTR?

Q4.1. Is there an interaction between the mention of price and the type of placement on the CTR?

Q4.2. Is there an interaction between promotion (gift, rebate or mention "free") and the type of placement on the CTR?

Control Variable

Size

The effect of size on advertising effectiveness has been widely studied in traditional media (Finn, 1988). Researchers showed that size improves memorization. Large advertisements occupy more vision field, which makes them more attention catching. Studies on print advertising confirmed that. Research on the Internet is not so conclusive: studies that examined the size of banners do not agree on the effect of the size. Chtourou and Chandon (2000) did not find any effects of the size on memorization. By contrast, Cho (1999) has shown that size explains the intention to click in situations of weak involvement. In a recent paper, Chandon and Chtourou (2001) showed that the size difference has a crucial role on the click-through rate between very small buttons and large banners but not within each of these categories.

In this study, we will consider two types of sizes: banners (234*60 and 468*60) versus smaller ads (234*30, 120*90, 120*60, 88*88). We investigate the following research question:

Q4.   Is there a relation between banner size and click-through rates?

In addition to the direct effect, we test the interaction between banner size and price information.

Tricky Banners

Several studies (especially professional ones: *www.bannertips.com*) suggest that use of banners simulating the operating system of the machine could enhance click-through rates. The same study says that the number of pages viewed after such a click is smaller than the ones observed for other banners, which suggests that this effect is mostly due to the user's novelty.

Q6.   Do banners using "tricks" have a better click-through rate than those which do not?

METHODOLOGY

Sample

Thanks to Wanadoo Régie, a web ad agency and one of the major actors in the Internet advertising market in France, we accessed a database of about 1,700 ad placements. A placement includes a banner placed in a given page for a specified period. The placements come from 77 announcers chosen from different sectors. These ad placements relate to about 1,000 different banners. These banners span the period from April 1999 to April 2000. It is necessary to have recent data since the attention paid to banners tends to decrease as the customer gets used to this type of ad. The effect of novelty vanishes gradually and thus the click-through ratio decreases (Lendrevie, 2000).

The web agency controls 7 web sites covering about 50% of the total French Internet audience. From our original database, we skipped the "barter/House" placements which are promotions for the agency itself. We also excluded placements with less than 25 impressions since we believe that they are trial placements and not effective ones. The sample includes 1,321 placements. In addition to these filters, we extracted four sectors which have not used promotion in their advertising. These sectors have no online transaction (see Appendix 1 for details). Final sample size was 1,134 insertions.

Description of Data

The preliminary analysis on the Click-through rates (CTR) reveals an asymmetrical shape of the distribution (skewness = 4.6, significantly > 0) which means that most of the CTR is concentrated in low values. The mean is 1.5. We must note here that this mean is not the one provided in market studies. The latest is computed by dividing the sum of the clicks by the sum of the placements, which corresponds in our study to the CTR mean weighted by the number of impressions. The weighted mean in our sample is 1.46. The standard deviation is 1.96 and the median is 0.89.

The logarithm of CTR is quite close to the normal distribution as seen in Figure 3.

Model

Since we want to test the effect of 6 categorical variables (price, promotion, banner size, tricky banners, placement and sector) to explain

FIGURE 2. Distribution of the Click-Through Rate

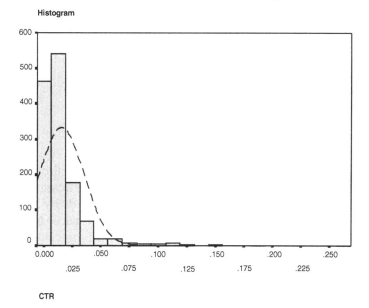

FIGURE 3. Distribution of LN(CTR)

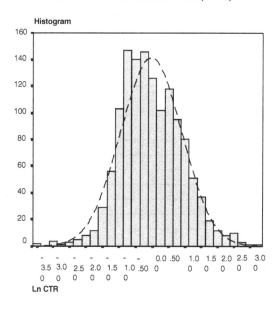

one numerical variable (the logarithm of click-through rate, better normally distributed than the click-through rate), we will use analysis of variance: the model included 6 direct effects and 4 interactions effects: promotion*size, promotion*placement, clear price*size and clear price*placement. We include one covariate: number of impressions, to control potential saturation effects. Altogether, we explain 45% of the total variance of the logarithm of CTR.

RESULTS AND DISCUSSION

The following ANOVA table (Table 1) shows that direct effect of both "mention of price" and "promotion" is not significant. These results seem to be consistent with those obtained by Degeratu, Rangaswamy and Wu (2000). The product category has a strong effect ($p < 0.001$ and $Eta^2 = .083$). The effect of number of impressions is non significant.

We note that price information has no uniform effect depending on the technique used: promotion has no significant linear effect. The effect of mentioning price is weak. It is not significant at the .05 tolerance level. Mentioning price actually tends to reduce the click-through rate.

TABLE 1. Variance Analysis of LN(CTR)

Tests of Between-Subjects Effects
Dependent Variable: LN(CTR)

Source	Type III Sum of Squares	df	Mean Square	F	Sig.	Eta
Promotion	.585	1	.585	1.246	.265	.001
Price mention	1.510	1	1.510	3.214	.073	.003
Placement (targeted vs non targeted)	3.921	1	3.921	8.344	.004	.007
Tricky banners	186.033	1	186.033	395.932	.000	.262
Sector	47.712	7	6.816	14.506	.000	.083
Size	33.514	1	33.514	71.326	.000	.060
PROMO * Size	2.237E-02	1	2.237E-02	.048	.827	.000
PROMO * Placement	1.986	1	1.986	4.228	.040	.004
Clear price * Placement	3.941	1	3.941	8.387	.004	.007
Clear price * Size	.142	1	.142	.302	.583	.000
Number of Impression	.315	1	.315	.671	.413	.001
Error	524.835	1117	.470			

a R Squared = .453 (Adjusted R Squared = .445)

The other effects are significant: using larger size and using tricky banner enhances CTR. Finally, CTR varies according to the product category. The effect of the number of impressions is insignificant. We notice that there is no significant moderating effect of size. Placement (linked to involvement) has a significant direct effect on CTR and a major impact on the effect of price information, as illustrated in Figure 5. Promotion, when used on a targeted placement, reduces the click-through rate (see Figure 4).

Promotions tend to enhance CTR in non-targeted placements, but it clearly decreases it in the case of targeted placements. Several explanations can be suggested.

It may be that involved users are more expert about the product category. Then they should rely more on their IRP and be less sensitive to the pricing argument.

It may be that "aggressive" promotions, frequent on the internet, are just not credible. For example, we found many unbelievable claims such as "a trip to Rome for 1 Franc" with a little footnote saying that this is the starting price of the auctions. Such techniques are unproductive in targeted placements where visitors are familiar with the product and then sensitive to the face validity of a claim.

FIGURE 4. The Effect of Promotion on CTR According to Type of Placement

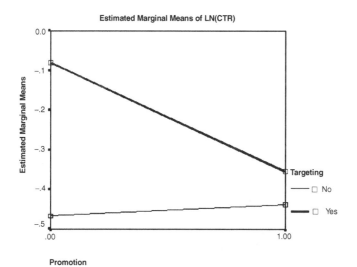

FIGURE 5. The Effect of Price Information on CTR According to Type of Placement

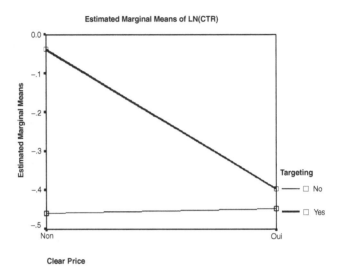

Clear Price

In addition, Table 1 shows that using tricky banners has an important effect on click-through rates. Two main explanations can be given for this phenomenon: the users' novelty makes them click thinking that the banner is a part of their operating system. Users are sensitive to the interactivity which seems to be allowed by the banner (especially when the banner simulates menus).

CONCLUSIONS AND LIMITS

Our study reveals a weak direct effect of the mention of price and no direct effect of price promotions on the click-through rate. Furthermore, the mention of price decreases the click-through rate for banners in a targeted placement. This applies also to promotions. They diminish click-through rates when appearing in targeted placements. The click-through rate depends on the product category. The click-through rate depends also on banner size and the use of tricks that trigger immediate response ("click here . . ."). These findings apply only to the immediate reaction of Internet users confronted with a banner. We do not study the delayed visit of the announcer's site and this is a major limit of our study.

Another limit to our work could be the way we infer the effect of price information: it may have been necessary to make comparisons between online and offline ads, following the method performed in previous studies (Degeratu, Rangaswamy and Wu, 2000). Furthermore, we have only behavioral data and thus we miss information on consumer's perception of price (ERP and IRP, indifference region).

Our results come from a natural experiment, on a large database, but this leads to unequal cell sizes. While our sample is rather large, it is not large enough to cross all sectors with our four variables of interest. For some sectors, we do not have banners that mention price or that use promotions. Further research is needed to focus on the individual perception of banners and then relate respondents' individual characteristics (age and gender) to their responsiveness to different type of promotions.

REFERENCES

Alba, J.W., Janiszewski, C., Lutz, R., Sawyer, A., Wood, S., Lynch J. & Weitz B. (1998) Achat interactif à domicile: quels avantages pour les consommateurs les distributeurs et les producteurs présents sur le marché électronique? *Recherche et Applications en Marketing, 13,* 79-102.

Alba, J.W., & Hutchinson, J.W. (1987) Dimensions of Consumer Expertise. *Journal of Consumer Research, 13,* 411-454.

Alba, J.W., Broniarczyk, S.M., Shimp, T.A., & Urbany, J.E. (1994) The Influence of Prior Beliefs; Frequency Cues and Magnitude Cues on Consumers' Perceptions of Comparative Price Data. *Journal of Consumer Research, 21,* 219-235.

Biswas, A., & Blair, E.A. (1991) Contextual Effects of Reference Prices in Retail Advertisements. *Journal of Marketing, 55,* 1-12.

Bourliataux, S. (2000) Marketing et Internet: le cas de la e-publicité. *Revue Française de Gestion* juin-août, 101-107.

Briggs, R., & Hollis, N. (1997) Advertising on the Web: Is There Any Response Before Click-Through? *Journal of Advertising Research, 37,* 33-45.

Chandon, P. (1994) Dix ans de recherche sur la psychologie et le comportement des consommateurs face aux promotions. *Revue Application en Marketing, 9,* 83-108.

Chang-Hoan, C. (1999) How Advertising Works on the WWW: Modified Elaboration Likelihood Model. *Journal of Current Research in Advertising, 27,* 33-50.

Cho, C. (1999) "How advertising Works on the WWW: Modified Elaboration Likelihood Model," *Journal of Current Issues and Research in Advertising,* No. 1.

Chtourou, M.S., & Chandon, J.L. (2000) Impact of Motion; Picture; Size on Recall; Consideration and Word-of-Mouth for Internet Banners, *2nd Marketing Science and the Internet Conference* Marshall School of Business–University of Southern California.

Copeland, M.T. (1923) The Relation of Consumers' Buying Habits to Marketing Methods. *Harvard Business Review, 1*, 282-289.

Degeratu, A.M., Rangaswamy, A., & Wu, J. (2000) Consumer Choice Behavior in Online and Traditional Supermarkets: The Effects of Brand Name, Price and Other Search Attributes. *International Journal of Research in Marketing, 17*, 55-78.

Desmet, P., & Zollinger, M. (1997) *Le prix: de l'analyse conceptuelle aux méthodes de fixation.* Economica Gestion–Paris.

Dreze, X. & Hussherr, F.X. (1999) Internet Advertising: Is Anybody Watching. Working Paper *http://www.xdreze.org/Publications/eye.html*

Dussart, Ch. (1999) La transparence on line. *Décisions Marketing, 17*, 67-72.

Engel, J.F., Blackwell, R.D., & Miniard, P.W. (1995) *Consumer Behavior–eighth ed.* The Dryden Press Harcourt Brace.

Fortin, D. (1997) *The Impact of Interactivity on Advertising Effectiveness in the New Media*, unpublished Ph.D. thesis, University of Rhode Island.

Harvey, B. (1997) "The expanded ARF model: Bridge to the Accountable Advertising Future. *Journal of Advertising Research*, Vol. 37-2 (March/April 1997), 11-21.

Helson, H. (1964) *Adaptation-Level Theory.* Harper & Row, New York.

Hoffmann, D.L., Novak, T.P., Chatterjee, P. (1998) Modeling the clickstream: Implication for web-based advertising efforts. *WP http://www2000.ogsm.vanderbilt.edu/*

Hussherr, F.X. (collective book) (1999) *La publicité sur Internet* Internet. Advertising Bureau–Dunod Paris.

Incentive magazine (2000) In "But Wait, There's More . . ." *Research Brief, 4* www.centerformediaresearch.com/cfmr_about.cfm

Infoseek (1996) Determinants of Click-Through Rates: Some Preliminary Results. *http://www.infoseek.com*

Janiszewski, C., & Lichtenstein, D.R. (1999) A Range Theory Account of Price Perception. *Journal of Consumer Research, 25*, 353-368.

Kelly, K.J. & Hoell, R.F. (1991) The Impact of Size, Color, and Copy Quantity on Yellow Pages Advertising Effectiveness. *Journal of Small Business Management*, Vol. 29, No. 4, pp. 64.

Lendrevie, J. (2000) Internet est-il doué pour la publicité? *Revue Française du Marketing, 177/178* 102-118.

Monroe, K.B. (1990) *Pricing: Making Profitable Decisions, 2nd ed.* McGraw Hill, New York.

Monroe, K.B., & Lee, A.Y. (1999) Remembering Versus Knowing: Issues in Buyers' Processing of Price Information. *Journal of the Academy of Marketing Science, 27*, 207-225.

Murphy, P.E., & Enis, B.M. (1986) Classifying Products Strategically. *Journal of Marketing, 50*, 24-42.

Naccarato, J.L. & Neuendorf, K.A. (1998) "Content Analysis as a Predictive Methodology: Recall Readership, and Evaluations of Business-to-Business Print Advertising." *Journal of Advertising Research*, 38(3), 19-33.

Onnein-Bonnefoy, C. (1997) Les bandeaux publicitaires sur Internet: mesures d'efficacité. *Décisions Marketing, 11*, 87-92.

Opinion Research Corporation International (2000) In "Comparison shoppers . . . " *Research Brief, 30 www.centerformediaresearch.com/cfmr_about.cfm*

Pavlou, P.A., & Stewart, D.W. (2000) Measuring the Effects and Effectiveness of Interactive Advertising: A Research Agenda. *Journal of Interactive Advertising, 1, http://jiad.org*

Rao, A.R., & Monroe, K.B. (1989) The Effect of Price; Brand Name; and Store Name on Buyers' Perceptions of Product Quality: An Integrative Review. *Journal of Marketing Research, 26,* 351-357.

Simester, D. (1995) Signalling Price Image Using Advertised Prices. *Marketing Science, 14,* 166-188.

Thaler, R. (1985) Mental Accounting and Consumer Choice. *Marketing Science, 4,* 199-214.

Urbany, J.E., Bearden, W.O., & Weilbaker, D.C. (1988) The Effect of Plausible and Exaggerated Reference Prices on Consumer Perceptions and Price Search. *Journal of Consumer Research, 15,* 95-110.

Zeithaml, V.A. (1988) Consumers Perceptions of Price, Quality and Value: A Means-End Model and Synthesis of Evidence. *Journal of Marketing, 52,* 2-22.

Zettelmeyer, F. (2000) Expanding the Internet: Pricing and Communications Strategies When Firms Compete on Multiple Channels. *Journal of Marketing Research, 37,* 292-308.

Zollinger, M. (1993) Le concept de prix de référence dans le comportement du consommateur: d'une revue de la littérature à l'élaboration d'un modèle prix de référence-acceptabilité. *Recherche et Applications en Marketing, 8,* 61-77.

APPENDIX
Sample Distribution Among the Experimental Cells

PROMO* sector Crosstabulation

Count

		Promotion		Total
		No	Yes	
Sector	Automotive	58	1	59
	General Distribution	53	5	58
	Spec Distrib	214	134	348
	Bidding - Group Buying	117	37	154
	Grocery*	62		62
	Computer	27	8	35
	Portal Media*	6		6
	Portal*	13		13
	Media	195	17	212
	B to B*	28		28
	Job Search services	36		36
	Tourism	117	69	186
	Telecom	83	19	102
	Others	19	3	22
Total		1028	293	1321

* these sectors have not been used for the analysis.

APPENDIX (continued)

Targeted* Promotion Crosstabulation
Count

		promotion		Total
		No	Yes	
Targeted	No	567	240	807
	Yes	284	44	328
Total		851	284	1135

Targeted* "mention price" Crosstabulation
Count

		Mention of price		Total
		No	Yes	
Targeted	No	502	305	807
	Yes	268	60	328
Total		770	365	1135

From the Tool to the Virtuality: Motivation and Styles of Internet Users: The Example of Seniors

Michelle Bergadaà

Mohamed Jamil Hebali

SUMMARY. The objective of this study is to understand the individual and Internet relationships through a qualitative study conducted by on-line questionnaires carried out on 131 Canadian and Swiss seniors.

We suggest a model which distinguishes three realities that the Internet encompasses for individuals.

The first reality is that of the Internet as a tool of communication. The second reality is that of the Internet as a device of interaction, and finally, the third reality is that of the Internet as a virtual world.

Four declared types of behaviors, or Internet users' styles, would be proposed in a second analysis. The study shows that any access to one of these options or to another seems to depend on factors that are specific to individuals, distinct from the more or less intensive use of this technology. *[Article copies available for a fee from The Haworth Document Delivery Service: 1-800-HAWORTH. E-mail address: <getinfo@haworthpressinc.com> Website: <http://www.HaworthPress.com> © 2001 by The Haworth Press, Inc. All rights reserved.]*

Michelle Bergadaà is Professor and Director of the Sales Observatory and Marketing Strategies (l'Observatoire de Vente et Stratégies du Marketing), HEC–University of Geneva (E-mail: Michelle.Bergadaa@hec.unige.ch). Mohamed Jamil Hebali is a Postgraduate Student of HEC–Management Studies–University of Geneva.

The authors are grateful to S. Belmiloud, C. De Donato, Mandula et B. Pianca, Geneva students, who collected the data used in this study.

The authors are also grateful to the FNRS, who financed this research.

[Haworth co-indexing entry note]: "From the Tool to the Virtuality: Motivation and Styles of Internet Users: The Example of Seniors." Bergadaà, Michelle, and Mohamed Jamil Hebali. Co-published simultaneously in *Journal of Euromarketing* (International Business Press, an imprint of The Haworth Press, Inc.) Vol. 11, No. 2, 2001, pp. 41-69; and: *Internet Applications in Euromarketing* (ed: Lynn R. Kahle) International Business Press, an imprint of The Haworth Press, Inc., 2001, pp. 41-69. Single or multiple copies of this article are available for a fee from The Haworth Document Delivery Service [1-800-HAWORTH, 9:00 a.m. - 5:00 p.m. (EST). E-mail address: getinfo@haworthpressinc.com].

KEYWORDS. Internet, virtual world, seniors, qualitative research

INTRODUCTION

The Internet, this new technology of information and communication induced transformation in every field of social, technical, industrial, commercial, cultural and psychological life.

The cyberspace, the virtual reality of dematerialized world between the imaginary and the real, will be likely to deeply influence our individual and collective actions.

Moreover, it will radically affect our societies (Rosnay, 1995; Levy, 1997). Some years ago, charmed journalists, sociologists and economists talked more and more frequently about this medium carrying individual and collective hope.

It's a fact, the Internet has invaded the world and every minute we see new Internet users connected to the web. The Internet can be practiced individually, within a group or in a social context.

The Internet involves changes in attitudes and behaviors of individuals who become genuine actors and creators of the network where they can freely express themselves because Internet receives from everybody and gives to everybody. New voices of expansion of the freedom of expression of citizenships, and of the access to knowledge are also blooming (Boutié, 1996; Levy, 1998; Mitchell, 1998; Hert, 1999).

However, what deeply distinguishes the researcher in marketing from his sociologist and philosopher fellows is the question that preoccupies him tirelessly. That is to understand in what way a transformation of society can directly, if not indirectly, influence the different social groups that constitute it. In view of expressions of a virtuality that, in a very little time, has invaded the media, the researcher in marketing must remain skeptical.

Before applying it indistinctly to the whole society, firstly, we have to understand what this concept of virtuality hides for the individuals. Then, we have to wonder about the possibility to segment this society accordingly on a socio-demographic basis or some other criterion.

So, only the researcher in marketing is capable of suggesting a conceptual model whose premises are theoretical but to which the reason for existing is its pragmatism, and eventually he can ask himself about the propagation speed of this studied phenomenon.

In this research, we are going about in a traditional way in marketing. First, the fact of choosing (as an object of research) the nature of virtuality accessible through the Internet as a subject of research naturally leads us to opt for a logic of discovery (Desphande, 1983). In fact, we are not in a framework of an emerging science as there are no more theoretical concepts that allow us to support a reasoning of a hypothetical deductive type in this field (Belk, 1998). Our methodology is of a qualitative type and we are proceeding in an inductive logic borrowed from ethnomethodology.

We have chosen to analyze a social group often defined as "latecomer" and who, nonetheless, occupies a more and more important place in society: The seniors; our analysis would lead us to induce the segmentation basis of this specific population, basis that is built on the motivation and the behaviors in view of Internet.

REVIEW OF LITERATURE

From the Use of Internet to Virtuality

The relationship between the individual and the Internet prospers through time. The revolution that the Internet brings about in our society is deep, and for some, more radical than any other tool. As, if it's true that man creates the tool, the tool shapes man, the new technologies will contribute in modeling a new relationship between man and the world.

Besides, according to the experience acquired from the evolution of interactivity with this machine, then he follows a total omission of context and thus a strong mental engagement (Csikszentmihaly, 1990; Hoffman and Novak, 1996; Millerand, 1999; Casalegno, 2000).

In addition, a first type of motivation makes the individual consider Internet as a tool of communication similar to others (TV, Phone, Fax . . .). At this level, the user obviously exists in a physical and real world since he conceives Internet only as a tool of communication sometimes simply more practical and/or more accessible than other classical ones.

However, a motivation of a different nature leads to the emergence of a genuine interaction created between the individual and Internet. The acquired experience, and the research of more valuable compatibility with the system put the individual in a relationship of natural interaction that goes hand in hand with the physical experiences previously lived (Holbrook, 1994). Over this point, two types of interactivity will be at issue. The first, the "interactive machine" will give the individual the possibility to participate in the content of an up-to-date broadcasted environment (Eveno and D'ibarne, 1997). The second, the "interactive person" will permit the user to get in a relation of exchange with other users (Hoffman and Novak, 1996b). The individual motivated to have access to this interactivity, must do his best to look for and obtain the information he wants, and the perceived value of the established interactivity is the obtained reward (Sterne, 1995).

Eventually, a third type of motivation, whose nature is of a superior order, will lead to a total involvement of the individual in the Internet. There will be a very high psychological and mental engagement that will place the individual inside a system of which he, himself, will be an integral part.

Some authors, from computer sciences origins, suggest that this virtual space will excite and speed up the consumers' senses in a way that they perceive the virtual environment as they perceive their physical one (Lauria, 1997; Biocca, 1997; Ellis, 1994). The individual will be able even to consider an action in his virtual environment as important as any other one in the real world (Stener, 1992). Here, it seems that two types of virtuality should be distinguished, too. The first argument deals with the real virtuality based, not on the emergence of the individual in virtuality, but on the cognitive argument. This argument defends the thesis of a virtual reality which is defined as the total emergence of the individual in an artificial and virtual world, in which the emphasis is placed on the power of the machine to usually better increase the experience of this virtuality (Buxton, 1994).

In our research, we want to understand whether these types of relationships which link individuals to the Internet clearly differ from one another and which type of motivation leads to one of these relationships or to another. The question is then to know how, in a dynamic way, Man-Internet relationship manifests itself. In other terms, how can the individuals progress or how do they want to do so?

Naturally, this question leads us to the analysis of restraints that curb the motivation to use Internet. The researches that have dealt with this problematic issue are rare. Boulaire and Balloffet (1999) have well studied the restraints and the motivations of using the Internet, but their study was based on determining the risks perceived even before coming in contact with the Internet. Their study showed the impact of technology on the motivation to use or not to use the Internet, in terms of motivation in relation to the innovation, to the novelty and to the perceived psychological, financial and technological risks.

In our research, we will notice how the individual, already a user, develops restraints linked to a specific motivation that makes him opt for a kind of relationship.

Seniors' Behavior

Generally speaking, the Internet is associated with youth, fashion. It's a way of life that charms with its dynamism, its worship of youth and its tolerance. As for innovators, in general, they are considered in marketing as the opposite of the seniors whom we have chosen to study (Dickerson and Gentry, 1983).

Indeed, age appears as one of the most important social demographic characteristics to explain the individuals resistance to new technologies (Rosen and Weil, 1995; Audit et al., 2000).

Besides, specific studies show the existence of a negative relationship between age and the use of certain technological innovations such as computers, automatic teller bank machines, calculators, video games, etc. (Kerschner and Chelsvig, 1981; Zeithaml and Gilly, 1987). And it's true because the elderly present a resistance to the use of new technology, a study of this population is important (Price, Arnould and Curasi, 2000). Moreover, we can wonder whether, in view of all the actual advertising publicity concerning the Internet, the senior's behaviours and needs in using this tool will not be likely to change. Because retired people are indeed concerned with a period of their life which is accompanied with changes in time and space organization, change in their social identity (Tamaro-Han, 1999), and the capability of innovation is also an expression of a need for stimulation (Rochrich, 1994). Nothing permits to believe that the seniors will be different from "others" in terms of their basic needs to discover all what is unknown and intriguing in their surroundings (Berlyne, 1960).

While dealing specifically with this seniors population, we wondered what could be the basis of their behaviours' segmentation in relation to this medium. The relationship between the individuals and an interactive technology will not only be that of manipulation, but further, than the concrete relation implied by its use, the values of this manipulation will contribute in shaping operative modes and new behaviours (Jouet, 1993).

Thanks to the acquired experience on the Net, the individual's behaviour will progress in order to adapt to and be more compatible with the whole system (Buxton, 1994; Hoffman and Novak, 1996; Holbrook, 1994). But none of the research studies carried out until now supports this hypothesis of a change in individual's behaviour because of the use of the Internet.

Moreover, this analysis ignores the influence of the individual's personal dimensions in the adoption of a specific behaviour on the Web. Nevertheless, the personality through concepts such as "self-efficiency" (Bandwa, 1997), will be a decisive factor of the individual's resistance towards innovations. This personality will then have a direct impact on the individual's propensity to adapt and adopt a new technology (Boulaire and Balloffet, 1999; Rosen et al., 1987) and it will negatively influence the rhythm of its circulation (Gatignon and Robertsen, 1985). In this context, nothing permits to presume that the seniors will be typical in terms of personality to the point that they also don't seek to be different while keeping their integrity in their social background (Frenkin, 1987).

In the present study, we will find out these various proposals by carrying out a survey on a population of elderly persons so as to verify what is the common motivation (probably due to specificities of age) in order to understand and determine the specific restraints of the motivation. Finally, we will find out the type of declared behaviour. This will lead us to wonder whether these behaviours towards the Internet result from a reflection of Personality and their lifestyle in the real world or, on the contrary, from a more or less intensive use of technology.

The Initial Model of Investigation

Our research set out to verify how the diverse proposals, resulting from the review of literature which is proceeding according to the following provisional model, articulate (Figure 1).

METHODOLOGY OF PRACTICAL RESEARCH

We have chosen to carry out our survey on-line because it was important that the interviewees had the leisure to develop specific attitudes towards this medium. In addition, in strict technical terms, the fact that the Internet makes the interactivity, the speed and the automation of the data processing become possible allows to obtain the qualitative information with a very low cost in comparison with the traditional qualitative methods (Aragon et al., 2000). If, the principal advantage of this type of investigation lies in the simplicity of implementation (Jones, 1999), and in the fact that the answers are fast and personalized, the

FIGURE 1. Tool of Communication in the Virtual World

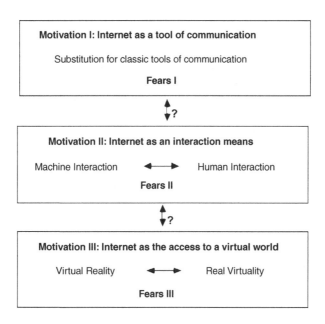

analysis of the investigation must be manually made, since each answer is expressed in a very personalized and free way. This intensive investigation was conducted between April and May, 2000.

Methodology of Data Collection

The methodology used in this online study has followed the rigorous stages in order to be ensured of the suitable representativeness of the data (Lescher, 1995; Galan and Vernette, 2000). Besides, like all studies of qualitative nature that proceed by the logic of inductive extraction, the choice of the sample is fundamental for its qualitative representation (Prust, 1987). We have proceeded in the following ways:

a. On an exploratory basis, three in-depth interviews from one hour to one hour and a half, were carried out with three retired persons (aged 58, 71 and 78 years old) and have allowed the development of an open questionnaire of nine questions (Appendix 1).

b. We have then defined our mother population to constitute our base of survey by having recourse to newsgroups frequently visited to target on our files (Adler et al., 1999). In the first newsgroups, "Pepper and Salt" (Canada), updating on January 1997, 159 correspondents were selected according to their age. In the second newsgroups, "Seniorweb" (Swiss), we have identified 320 seniors indicating to communicate in French.

c. The questionnaires were sent by email in an attached document. The attached letter identified clearly the source of the investigation (university professor) and called upon the feeling of co-operation of the interviewees towards precise objectives, as well as the deadline of answer. Finally, the message of request was individualized (e.g., *"Dear Mr Tremblay"*).

d. 144 answers were received, i.e., a rate of positive answers of 30%, including 131 analyzable within the time limits given to study. These important figures prove that the study aroused the interest of these seniors whose age varies between 57 years and 84 years, i.e., 67 years old on average. Please note that 6 of them had preserved a part-time activity; all the others were true retired people.

e. The data reception being made by email, each received answer was controlled before being analyzed to check its origin (only one doubtful case concerning the sender was eliminated).

Methodology of Data Analysis

The interpretation of the collected data was carried out through a process of analysis of traditional interactive and systematic content (Churchill and Wertz, 1985; McCracken, 1988b; Clairbrone and Ozanne, 1990; Bergadaà and Nyeck, 1995). The data were analyzed in an independent way by many researchers, then the whole of these punctual analyses was put in a general interpretative framework. During the comparison of the results, the exchanges between researchers were likely to deepen and to enrich the proposals by intersubjective validation. We have implemented the analysis in three principal phases:

a. We have started with a "floating" reading of the three basic interviews in order to have the first intuitions towards the formulation of the work questions by keeping induction separating the particular from the general (Bardin, 1977).

b. A structuring traditional analysis of content was then conducted on the basis of 135 pages of quotes received from our interviewees. This analysis permits us to understand the nature of the principal motivations guiding the seniors in their relation with the Internet. Here, we start from each one's particular elements we gradually collect to obtain the more precise description of the suggested categories and the semiotic "springs" animating them. This analysis has led us to verify the hypothesis resulting from the review of literature as which the motivation towards Internet could be of different nature according to whether the individual tends towards "a tool of communication," "a means of interaction" or an "access to virtuality." And since all motivations induce some restraints, we have sought to understand the latter. We will see in the following pages to what extent the nature of motivation and restraints are in fact closely connected.

c. Proceeding our analysis, we have observed, then induced how each nature of motivation was translated into terms of declared behavior. The same procedure of analysis and contents enabled us to induce three principal "styles of Internet-users": "functional Internet-users," "curious Internet-users" and "social Internet-users."

d. Have validated our results by comparing the two samples (Canadian and Swiss) in order to verify whether the suggested model applies, or not, to different cultural contexts.

e. In order to facilitate the reading of our results, we proceeded in the traditional way of qualitative research, i.e., by using characteristic verbatim to illustrate each part of the final model suggested then in an integral model (Wolcoot, 1990).

RESULTS OF THE FIRST ANALYSIS: MOTIVATION AND RESTRAINTS

After having noted that there was no reason to consider *a priori* the seniors as a population distinct from other Internet-users by the simple criterion of age, the question was: What can motivate the individuals in their relation with the Internet? We tried to understand how the Internet, as new technology and new medium, was perceived. We have actually found the three categories which our theoretical model proposed about the Internet that can be considered as:

- a tool of communication, where the Internet-users' behavior remains rather passive (it receives information; it transmits information).
- a means of interaction, where the individual really seeks to create an interaction and it's this interaction that gains some value;
- an access to a virtual world, where the individual turns to new methods having relation with his environment.

Please note that this first reading of the collected data also reveals the six categories of perceived risks proposed by Boulaire and Balloffet (1999): the financial risk of the technology which is costly (e.g., *"My invoice of telephone bill increased"*), the functional risk related to the failures of technology or its complexity (e.g., *"What annoys me, it is that you find almost nobody to help you if you have a problem"*), the social risk or coldness and the disintegration of the social bond associated with technology (e.g., *"I like to communicate on-line with people whom I do not know. Unfortunately there are many fools, patients and company"*), the risk related to the safety and the attack of the private life or the reign of the technology which extends (e.g., *"the need for giving his personal address to have access to certain documents allows the solicitants to flood us with publicity"*), the perceived psychological and physical risks or the alienating power of technology (e.g., *"I spend there too much time instead of devoting myself to other activities"*). On the contrary to what the study of Boulaire and Balloffet (1999) could suppose, these restraints do not prevent Internet use. This type of fear is too general to allow an understanding of their impact on the modifications of the felt motivations. However, the second traditional analysis of contents hereafter clarifies this dynamic aspect of the connection motivation-restraints towards the Internet.

Motivation and Restraints Related to the Tool of Communication

When the Internet is perceived as a tool of communication, the individuals conceive it as being more or less efficient in comparison with their needs, and are motivated by its utility aspect. Here, the individual uses the Internet to replace other traditional means of communication such as the fax, the telephone, the television, the newspapers, etc. Nevertheless, he does not modify the organization of his activities because of the use of the practical tool that the Internet represents for him. For example:

I mainly use Internet for the results of sports and/or some news and for an itinerary of journey or of the problems of general interest. Personally, I do not think that we should consider Internet as a toy or a machine to surf the Net, but I think of a major utility for the future. I do not have special attraction concerning Internet, if it is not perhaps the speed to send and receive mail or external contacts. I have a bad manual writing, thus illegible!!! Internet does not change many things in my life, if it only allows me, for example, to converse with you or exchange mail with friends. But I attached there some importance in the fact that I make my brain work a little. (h.72 a little. ex. commercial, Swiss)

We wondered about the reasons that could restrain individuals of this category from extending their relation with Internet towards other types of relation. The principal restraint that prevents them from reaching new motivations is related to the functionality and the complexity of the technology of access to Internet. For example:

*What displeases me and slows me down in Internet is my lack of deep knowledge in computer sciences. In the framework of my previous job, I had always to do nearly the same tasks and I remain, as my daughter said, "perfectly computer illiterate" and I am plagued when I am unable to solve a problem by myself. I was unable to open your attached file. And (as) proof of my perfect lack of knowledge of computer sciences, I do not know how to make it readable. **I looked at only lines and lines of small square.** (f. 62 A., accountant, e.g., Switzerland)*

For other persons, what restrains them is the relation with the way of thinking required by the Internet in order to overtake this motivation of utility type. For example:

Surfer does not give me any pleasure. I cannot use it as an encyclopedia where I can easily spend many hours. Moreover, I do not like to read a vertical text. I prefer to lay it down on the table what (sic.) enables me to underline or to note remarks down. Having progressive glasses, I am obliged to remain in front of the almost motionless screen to arrive at the good focus. The research engines should work on a simple and uniform system to reach at desired information. For fully profiting from Internet it is necessary to apply a completely different way of thinking and to formulate a research which, for me, is too abstract. I do not see, for me, the interest to obtain information in this way as long as I still have the traditional means at my disposal. Moreover, due to the fact that anyone can launch a text on the Net, the user must make a sorting of what is valid and correct–but if I ask for information it is precisely because I do not know the answer–so how can I sort? (65 A., e.g., executive secretary, Switzerland)

Thus, these persons have little chance to be motivated by the interactive relation which the Internet also allows, so much that the use of this media calls for a new thought and operating mode, a cognitive "internal" revolution which they do not seem ready to do.

Motivation and Restraints Linked to Means of Interaction

We find some individuals who, having overcome the preceding restraints, develop a motivation centered towards the search for an amplified interaction with their environment. We find each of them having an expression of the "human interactivity" and "machine interactivity" proposed in our initial model. It does not mean any more, indeed, a simple exchange of information, as in the preceding case. Here Internet is a means which, by supporting this interaction, creates the foundations of an actors' community which would not have had, if not, any reason to meet, to enter into relation of exchange and, finally, to provide the basis of a meta-communication (Bateson, 1984; Watzlawick, 1978; Wittezaele and Garcia, 1992). As follows:

In this moment, I use it for my courses of French, history and English. Besides, I send the reports of my party (PDC) by E-mails to our members and I communicate with my family and others. Moreover, I make my payments by banking Internet. I know that Internet will change the academic education. But will it be the social revolution as in XIXe century? I do not know. We will see. I like to spend more as nice hours to excavate in various categories, to look as much as possible and to learn the most possible. But I am also irritated, when I cannot get through. I find it wonderful to be able to ask questions to anyone, at any hour. (h., 60 A., e.g., professor of the secondary, Switzerland)

The following question was to understand why individuals who "surf" rather easily so that Internet can take a value of interaction means with their environment did not change radically in this cyberspace which does one of the newspapers. We discovered two types of characteristic fears in these people: the personal or social loss of control in the relation "Virtual world–real world." Thus, the first fear is that of "no personal control" and the intrusion in the private sphere. For example:

> *It is an extraordinary medium. I think, however, that it is impor-*
> *tant that we accept to discipline "ourselves" as for as use. I know*
> *a friend who spends approximately 15 hours each day on Internet.*
> *Consequence: the couple is in serious difficulties! Internet puts us*
> *in relation to the world, however, one has tendency, if one does not*
> *pay attention, to neglect the people who are close to us.* (h. 67 A.,
> ex. Teacher, Canada)

For many other people, the restraints are related to the absence of social control of the interactions which seem to prevent them from really entering into the virtual world, as for example:

> *What displeases me is that some profit for circulating on the Net*
> *(pedophiles, robbers, liars, swindling sites) . . . but like all the me-*
> *dia there is the loss of control. The most tedious on the Net is the*
> *difficulty to catch the concerned persons. Even worse, it is said*
> *that I can preserve my data in certain sites and make use of it for*
> *purposes which I do not know.* (h. 79 A., e.g., tally commercial,
> Suisse)

Thus, many Internet users motivated by the interactions that Internet allows to develop are afraid, at the same time, of the interaction nuisance which would go to any azimuth. Especially, they fear to get over a fundamental stage which could lead them to lose ground in relation to the concrete reality of their daily life.

Motivation and Restraints Related to the Access to a Virtual World

Here Internet is perceived as a true method of communication significantly differing from all that the individuals knew before. Surely this constitutes a true rupture, but it is surprising to see the term of "virtual world" treated in a journalistic or sociological way as if Internet *imposed* its "virtuality" to mankind.

However, we found in our sample only the quarter of Internet users who, in contrast to those of the two previous categories, are motivated by the fact of being located "in" Internet. These people often communicate through interface which is their reflection, often creating personal Web pages, imagining the virtual world of tomorrow, and talking about global language, etc. We found individuals who seem to be led by the search for a "real virtuality," and others for a "virtual reality." But this distinction did not appear useful for the understanding of the individual reasons. On the other hand, we clearly find in the comments of each one, that beyond new means of communication, Internet has the capacity to modify the current social order of knowledge, and thus the "homo sapiens," idea developed by authors such as Michel Serres, for instance (1997). For example:

A great invention! What I like is to be able to access rather quickly to all information in a way more practical than the encyclopedias and in less costly way. What attracts me is the possibility of surfing whenever I want even at 3 a.m. to fill an insomnia or in the afternoon . . . I only have to connect myself and at any hour I can come in contact with somebody in the world. Yes, I think that Internet can be regarded as a form of social revolution. Why? Because, in my opinion, in a positive way it allows the isolated persons going out of their isolation (often the old and/or the retired persons). However, it should not be forgotten that sometimes Internet can have a negative effect on the life of the people neglecting their close relations in order to surf the Net . . . I think that Internet is a wonderful invention and realization of the Man. That it is also something we will leave to the future generations. (h. . . . 63 a., e.g., Canadian insurance advisor)

For the individuals living in this virtual world in a rather relaxed manner, there are always fears but they do not constitute real and effective restraints. For example:

What slows me down a little are the advertising headbands. In order to survive, certain sites need to use this means, but sometimes it is nevertheless too much, therefore I put them aside. There is, of course, several sites which I do not like, but it is related to subjects which are not interesting to me in the life. I leave them also aside. It must be for all the world. (f of it. 69 A., time-partial accountant, Switzerland)

On the other hand, others while personally joining (becoming a member of) to the virtual world express fears for "the others" and call for the invention of a certain social order. For example:

> *I believe that Internet can be used to humanize Humanity or destroy it . . . I believe that we should try to create, on the international level, a monitoring and Audit Board in order to stop all kinds of the abuses flooding into the system. Even better, I believe that the best specialists including the young people–"a generation of computer sciences geniuses"–should look into this question which appears to me fundamental for the future of Internet.* (76 years Roman Catholic priest. Canadian of Quebec)

Conclusion of the Analysis of the Motivations and Restraints

We did not discover any significant connection between the nature of the motivations, which led the seniors of the sample to stay before their screen, and the duration of this relation, which varied from two to fifteen hours per week. We have observed a significant distinction between the three types of motivation: the tool, the interactivity and the virtuality. It does not seem obvious that the increasing use of the machine in the "mechanical" way, as suggested by many authors, modifies the behaviors in time. But it is certain that the individuals are able or not to overcome some restraints.

STYLES OF DECLARED BEHAVIOR
REGARDING THE INTERNET

In this second analysis, we set out to analyze the type of declared effective behavior. For each of the three preceding types of motivations, we induced four styles of similar behaviors. The question obviously is to know why this similarity of behavior was found whereas the underlying motivations were so different.

If the present research does not allow to verify it, we will put forward a hypothesis according to which the individuals' personality leads them to adopt a style of specific behavior against any object of communication (here Internet). We have thus found, by induction on the basis of their declaration of behavior, that the individuals expressing their interest in carrying out their current operations as well as possible, and thus choosing the mainly "functional" behaviors. Other Internet-users declare to let their curiosity push them, obtain information, discover new ideas or people. A third category is especially stated to guide by the social relation that the Internet makes possible. Finally, some individuals tend to implement the shifts from a functional behavior to a curious then social behavior.

Style of Behaviors and the Tool of Communication

When the Internet is represented as the tool of communication which motivates the individuals (53% of the sample), we met four declared distinct behaviors. There are 7 functional Internet users, 19 curious Internet users, 20 social Internet users, and 24 Internet users declaring a behavior of the mixed type.

Functional Internet Users

In fact, by a methodological means, we have found only very few persons whose declared behavior towards Internet is that of the use of a tool for functional aims (to communicate with us is not very "useful" for them). Here is an example of verbatim:

> *I use Internet to make enquiries (about time, No of Tel.), for my banking transactions and postal transfer, learn and from time to time with pleasure. But it is a trend; this does not replace anything or it simply makes service and keeps me amused for the lonely evenings. (h. 70 A., ex. Engineer)*

Curious Internet Users

The second category of declared behavior raised here is that of the people for whom the Internet is a means of discovering new knowledge. For example:

> *I came to Internet by curiosity, the press spoke about it; it was new, I wanted to see, it was the whole beginning. As a member of a video list, I find there the solution to many editing problems. Internet it is the new occasion to exchange to understand. In my opinion we did not sufficiently speak about incomprehension, clashes and conflicts. It is an immense opening towards the world*

in all its forms, human, professional, etc. . . . At the end of my working life, Internet had not yet existed in the current form. That forced me to make my brain working, to understand, to be lost in order to find out the functioning, the searched subject, the solution for my troubles. (h. 67 A., e.g., insurance advisor, Europe)

Social Internet Users

The third category of declared behavior here is that of the people whose level of behavior is mainly social. If Internet did not exist, they would undoubtedly find out many other ways to communicate with the others. Here, Internet gives them especially an increased social space. The following verbatim characterizes the passion for this new tool. For example:

*Internet came to me without my realization. I still use other differ-ent forms of communication. With Internet, we do not always go to the better, but in any case to the easier and unfortunately to the more passive . . . However, the possibilities are so extraordinary: **the world is within the reach of keyboard!** It contributes to make my retirement very pleasant . . . The Americans did not make only bad inventions . . . the proof! And Bill Gates deserves well his en-tire billions! Flexibility of execution, the rapidity and the diversity. And when I "chat" with young ladies of Paris or Montreal and Geneva, I had only 25 years. The economy of the radio and the telephone communications is also very important.* (h. 62 years, ex-contractor of construction, Canada)

Mixed Internet Users

Finally, other Internet users, while having a behavior of the func-tional type, use the three possibilities of Internet apparently without preference for one or the other. For example:

For me, the Internet is a kind of challenge to update what occurs, and to prove that I am still able to learn something. First of all, Internet maintains a relation with my correspondents by email (friends, family). Then, I consult the press almost each day. I travel quite a lot, and seek information on the countries that I will visit. And finally, I "surf" from time to time to find the sites recom-

mended either by my close relations or by newspapers. Internet has a social function only through email. For the other functions, I think that the people using Internet each day for a long time terribly isolate themselves and become unsociable. (H., 62 years, e.g., accountant, Canada)

Styles of Behaviors Towards Means of Interaction

Since it is the means of interaction, that the Internet represents, which motivates the individuals (27% of the sample), we have met four declared distinct behaviors. There are 2 functional Internet users, 11 curious Internet users, 11 social Internet users, and 12 Internet users declaring a behavior of the mixed type.

Functional Internet Users

Always guided by the will to find practical solutions to their problems, individuals of this category completely appreciate the feedback that the Internet authorizes, which allows them to organize themselves effectively. For example:

For our journeys, reservations of hotels, search for shows, concerts or other useful documents to organize a trip. Why? Because we can find there the majority of the answers to our questions and perhaps make new knowledge. This possibility is very practical to make choices or to take options which we would not have thought of before. (F 60 years ex. Assistant of direction, Switzerland)

Curious Internet Users

Here also the concept of exchange seems to be the key to individuals' active behavior. Their spontaneous curiosity seems often to be greatly increasing. For example:

I use Internet to prepare my trips like Indonesia and Vietnam last year and Borneo this year, to make me informed of what occurs in France for expatriates, and for the elections in France. As I am hard of hearing, abandoned, it is a clear improvement. I like to dialogue on line with people whom I do not know and obtain the information that I can find despite the fact that I speak only French. I can read the newspapers of my original area. I find the change for any country in the world on the websites of the countries which I visited and that I am happy to find. I am also a member of a list in Indonesia, my adored country, and I was able to follow day by day the revolution which relieved Suharto as well as the tragic events of Timor. I have learned Internet by myself. Still my curiosity! (F 68 A., e.g., government official, Canada)

Social Internet Users

When the Internet would be perceived as a means of communication, the implicit need is one of membership, where the individual seeks to create social relations which gives him the feeling of living in the middle of a group of individuals who share with him a well-precise spatial and temporal dimension. Here, the individuals take part in group discussions, chats and forums. And we find the concept of a relation starting with a need of conversation where each individual seeks to express himself, in order to create this community's own values. For example:

> *I have as provider AOL version 5.0, and all works tremendously well. I use mainly Internet, for I discovered the power which could have in the transmission of documents and mail. The ability to join anybody, anywhere in the world at any time, was something I have never thought of. I have been an Internet user for six years. The fax is already out-of-date, and that is not the end!! Yes, I sincerely think that Internet is a social revolution, in all the fields . . . I think that Internet is really adapted to our XXIe century, the world is moving, receives information very quickly, reacts in the same way . . . Internet has allowed me to discover many friends in the world (Canadian, Swiss, Japanese, German, American). We do not all speak French well, but since we have written to one another we have meanwhile made a great progress.* (h.64 A., ex-chief of manufacture, in a company of clothes industry, Canada)

Mixed Internet Users

After all, if they appreciate all the exchanges that the access to Internet provides, these people would like to reinforce more the interactivity. Engaged in a permanent process of exchange they do not appreciate that these relations are not more fluent. For example:

> *that permits to make fast and cheap exchanges. The only restraint, in my view point, is that one can communicate only from his house*

(I dream of hotels putting computers at the disposal of their customers for their electronic mail, rather than TV). I also watch the news, the weather forecasts, the programs of museums and the schedules of railways. Preparing a next trip to Portugal and my wife speaking Portuguese, I thus was able to obtain schedules, information as well as splendid photographs. I once practiced a purchase of a book. It took me one month to receive it, because of a strike of the post offices in France. (h. 60, e.g., bank clerk, Swiss)

Styles of Behaviors in View of the Access to a Virtual World

When the Internet is represented as a virtual world which motivates the individuals (19% of the sample), we have met four declared distinct behaviors. There is only one functional Internet user, 8 curious Internet users, 7 social Internet users, and 9 Internet users declaring a behavior of the mixed type.

Functional Internet Users

It may seem strange to find functional people in a virtual world. However, these pragmatic individuals exist. . . . We can wonder whether the intellectuals speaking about virtuality are not so much (intellectual) that they forget that virtuality can also be fully approached by people with the pragmatic spirit. For example:

I have used the program here to have contacts and to exchange photographs with the whole world, for example EU, Canada, Brazil, Virgin Island, Tasmanie, etc. I have never attended a course of computer, but I have a friend who sometimes helped me from time to me. Today I make my payments directly by the bank and I follow my banking accounts (up to date deposits with values, etc.) Super! I have a great pleasure to write letters with heads of photographs according to the occasion; however before this I did not like to write letters manually. The possibility of creating beautiful personalized pages fascinates me. I spend probably an average of half an hour everyday on the computer (what a word "computer") when I think of the disorder in here! I also often use email to send photographs. (h. 71 A., ex. Punched-card operator, Switzerland)

Curious Internet Users

The curious individuals having approached the banks of virtuality are so enthusiastic that it is difficult to stop them from talking. They are ecstatic and it is difficult to choose in the glowing terms the quote which best describes their degree of inspiration. All have an emotional vocabulary when they speak about what seems to be the discovery of their life. For example:

> . . . *Like all the trades of the world, a training was necessary, before being able to sail between the five continents. At the beginning, the dispersion does not favor the effectiveness. Quickly the method and the organization take again their rights and override the irrational one with the satisfaction of the sacrosanct productivity. Internet has become a friend, a confidante, an educationalist who explains the access to the knowledge, a light to the spirit, a companion and sometimes a confidante. The rapidity, the access to the most important data bases of the cultural sites. . . . For a long time, I believed that it was only one new advertising modern gadget. One day I crossed the threshold of Internet to **discover that it was not the supervised hunting of the new technologies' maniacs.** It was necessary for me to go back to English.* (h. 68, e.g., Agricultural engineer Europe)

Social Internet Users

With the social Internet users, we find the same affectivity that we have met with the previous one. But for them, virtuality and planet are often synonymous. For example:

> *I have discovered wonderful things and I have taken great care to send my own compositions to various places of the world. To enter in communication with the world, planet is essentially what fascinates me. The fact of surfing enables me to perfect my knowledge, and to learn from others. Yes, by the fact that it brings people closer, various movements. It also makes it possible to confront the values, to know the various ethnic groups to better know them and thus to better understand and to appreciate them. I sincerely think that people everywhere cannot be the same now because of this medium . . . Instead of becoming a knitting mammies or cake-maker, I have became a "informatics mammies," according*

to the terms of my grandson for whom I solve "difficult" mysteries of Black and Mortimer. (f. 67 A. ex. Teacher, Canada)

Mixed Internet Users

While hearing about the Internet users having such a virtual behavior towards the Internet, we wonder whether we haven't simply changed to a science-fiction world where "virtual" and "dreams" are strangely joined. However, they do not seem completely fooled and fear only that the "ideal" world which they touch with the finger would be "corrupt" by some perversion. The following quote characterized this state of mind:

> *Henceforth, each individual on earth can freely have access to all what he wants of information, without any restriction. He can listen to the music of his choice, discover museums and art galleries, consult works in national libraries or read the newspapers and the magazines of the whole world. Moreover, and that is essential, he can communicate all over the planet, either by email, or by the forums of discussion, or by the "chat." Thus, he comes out of his loneliness and becomes a citizen of the world in the strict meaning of this term. After such a panegyric, you realize that I think all the best of Internet. . . .The discovery of websites well-built and interesting, and the visit (sic.) of museums. Finally, the listening to the desired music with the possibility of downloading satisfy me the most. Without restriction? No. Anonymity seems to stimulate certain correspondents in the crado kind.* (h. 83 A., ex tally commercial, Suisse)

Conclusion of the Behaviors' Analysis

With the exit of this analysis, we must balance our initial hypothesis according to which the personality of individuals would induce specific behaviors. Admittedly, we have systematically found our four types of significant and principal behaviors such as functional Internet users' style, a curious style, a social style, and a mixed style in each of our three categories of relations with Internet, i.e., the tool, the interaction and the virtuality.

We are able now to propose an integrative model (Figure 2) of the results regarding these styles of behaviors related to the motivations and restraints on the motivation of the previous paragraph.

FIGURE 2. The Model of Motivations, Restraints and Styles of Internet Users

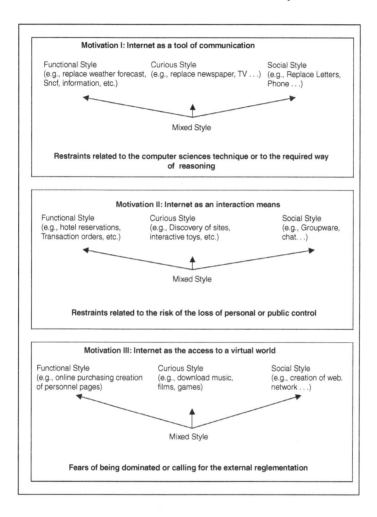

CONCLUSION

Among the expansion of current articles concerning the capacity of attraction of the Internet on individuals, and the fascination which it exerts, there exist radically different prospects. Thus, these reasons vary from a social and philosophical nature, which are advanced in comparison with the cyberspace (e.g., Rosnay, 1995), to the attempts of explanations based on individual cognitive reasons (Alba et al., 1997). If this object of research is approached by its technological component, the thesis of the personal characteristics likely to be factors of resistance to a new technology is advanced (Clegg et al., 1997; Ram, 1987; Emmanouilides and Hammond, 2000); or, on the contrary, the factors of adoption and adaptation to the innovation are put forward (Gatignon and Robertson, 1985). As for the rare marketing studies which analyze the Individual-Internet interaction, they fall under a logic of adoption or non-adoption and most often only for one aspect of the Internet, generally E-trade (Boulaire and Balloffet, 1999).

Our specific qualitative study led among a homogeneous sample in terms of age and occupation (seniors) enabled us to identify, on the one hand, how the Internet was perceived in a general way by the whole of the Individuals and, on the other hand, to induce our analysis of the individuals' differentiated profiles. This comprehensive study allows us to induce a conceptual model clearly distinguishing a motivation about the use of a communication tool, another about the interaction and the third concerning the aspiration towards a virtual world. With each of these types of motivations, the powerful personal restraints were associated. Our model also proposes four styles of Internet users which appear founded more on reasons pointing out the individual personalities, rather than explanations related to a more or less important use of the medium. Yet, if we have discovered that individuals could be functional, curious or social at the same time within each category, we have not encountered one individual case being systematically curious (or functional or social) in a relation with the Internet which would have been at the same time about the tool and of the interaction and the virtuality.

Restraints felt by individuals to move from an "Internet–tool of communication," to an "Internet–means of interaction," and to an "Internet–virtual world" seem powerful. Thus, at the end of this research, nothing allows us to suppose that one day, all human beings will have changed radically in the cyber world. Nevertheless, the photography we have taken in this research authorizes us to propose that the Internet can have at least three distinct realities that individuals choose to or choose not to integrate into their daily life. Please note that these "realities" have the roots which also draw from explanations of powerful epistemological order. Between the objective and the concrete world, served by the tool, the interaction world preached by the School of Palo Viola of communication, and the virtual culture put forward by philosophers such as Michel Greenhouses, the individual has the choice. Still he must decide to question himself about the "why?" of his choice of reality and to discover in what way does this "reality" integrate with the culture, with the personality, and with the way of life of the individuals.

The question of the robustness of this model obviously arises now. Note that, first of all, no significant difference could be found in terms of representativeness of our categories between our Canadian and Swiss seniors. And yet, the price of communications largely differs from one country to another and we had thought that, perhaps, this would influence the motivations and behaviors. Actually, it seems that only the weekly time that the Canadians devote in the winter to the Internet seems much higher than that reserved by the Swiss ones. Like the following story of a 71-year-old woman: *"Internet yet does not really change anything in my life, but when one knows the winters of Quebec . . .! The next will be perhaps less long and hotter thanks to this new way of communication."*

In fact, three principal motivations regarding this medium and four styles of Internet users seem "intuitively" in conformity with those which could be the attitudes and styles of the whole population. However, it would be interesting to check our proposal for a nature of motivation and styles of Internet users by making a complementary study among other samples of the population for the generalization of our model.

In the social level, one of the reasons of the rapid appropriation of Internet by the seniors of our sample is related to the time they dispose to adapt to this new medium. The passage from an active life to the life of a retiree is accompanied by changes that Tamaro-Hans (1999) defines according to three principal axis. First of all, the passage to a concept of active time to inactive time, which involves a reorganization of their spare time. Then, the change of the places of activity is replaced to that of the working place. Lastly, a modification of the social role: new forms of family relations, professional relations and social relations. Thus, the hypothesis that we should propose would be that of seniors who seek new external relations and for new activities to define another social identity in a "retirement" would be one privileged moment to discover Internet (ex., *"My son said: you will become impossible and difficult, the best is to give you something to occupy yourself now"*). In any case *The Guardian* of Friday March 30 2001: *"Internet is becoming something for the seniors, more than for the young people, according to a study of the Barclay bank."*

This issue has to be followed, because, as we all know, there is a continuous increase of persons retiring in good health and good financial conditions. These seniors could become a target of choice for the creators of websites and e-commercial actors, even though they are more difficult to allure at first; they can also be more faithful than Internet professionals who could become their partners (Peterson, Balasubramanian and Bronnenberg, 1997; Nicovitch and Cornwell, 1999). Whatever the argument which governs the research on relations on the Net, it provides to a population particularly sensitive to these dimensions the unbelievable possibility to escape from the uniqueness of the localization in space and the linearity of a time, which is not always favorable for them.

BIBLIOGRAPHY

Adler A., Ito M., Linde C., Mynatt E. et O'Day V. (1999), Final Report: Broadening Access: Research for Diverse Network Communities, http://www.senoirnet.org/research/9911.sht

Alba J., Lynch J., Weitz B., Janiszewski C., Lutz R., Sawyer A. et Wood S. (1997), Interactive Home Shopping Consumer, Retailer and Manufacturer Incentives to participate in Electronic Marketplaces, *Journal of Marketing*, 61, 38-53.

Aragon Y., Bertrand S., Cabanel M. et Le Grand H. (2000), Méthode d'enquête par Internet: Leçons de quelques expériences, *Décision Marketing*, 19, janv.-avril, 29-37.

Audit A., Danard N. et Tassi P. (2000), Age et diversité des comportements des téléspectateurs, *Décision Marketing*, 19, janv.-avril, 61-74.

Bandura A. (1977), *Social Learning Theory*, Prentice-Hall.

Bardin L. (1977), *L'analyse de contenu*, Presses Universitaires de France.

Bateson G. (1984), *La nature de la pensée*, Edition du Seuil, Paris.

Belk R. W. (1988), Possessions and the Extended Self, *Journal of Consumer Research*, 15 (september), 139-168.

Bergadaà M. et Nyeck S. (1995), Une analyse qualitative comparée des motivations des consommateurs et producteurs de théatre, *Recherche et Application en Marketing*, 10, 4, 27-45.

Berlyne D. E. (1960), *Conflict, Arousal and Curiosity*, New York, MacGraw Hill.

Biocca F. (1997), The cyborg's dilemma: Progressive embodiment in virtual environment, *Journal of Computer Mediated Communication*, Internet ref: *http://www.ascusc.org/jcmc/vol3/issue2/biocca2.html*

Boulaire C. et Balloffet P. (1999), Freins et motivations à l'utilisation d'Internet: une exploration par le biais de métaphores, *Recherche et Application en Marketing*, 14, 1, 21-39.

Boutié P. (1996), Ceci tuera-t-il cela? Les médias numériques vont-ils révolutionner la communication? *Revue Française de Marketing*, 156, 5-11.

Buxton W. (1994), *Human Skills in Interface Design, Interacting with Virtual Environments*, Lindsay Macdonald and John Vince, eds. Chichester: John Wiley and Sons, 1-12.

Casalegno F. (2000), Aux frontières du virtuel et du réel: Entretien avec Sherry Turkle sur l'impact social des nouvelles formes des communication en ligne, *Sociétés*, 68, 2, 9-18.

Churchill S. D. et Wertz F. J. (1985), An Introduction to Phenomenology for Consumer Research: Historical, Conceptual and Methodological Foundations, *Advances in Consumer Research*, 12, 550-554.

Clairbone A. et Ozanne J-L. (1990), The Meaning of Custom-Made Homes: Home As a Metaphor for Living, *Advances in Consumer Research*, 17, M. E. Goldberg, G. Gorn et R. W. Poolay eds., Provo, UT: Association for Consumer Research, 367-374.

Clegg C., Carey N., Dean G., Hornby P. et Bolden R. (1997), User's Reactions to Information Technology: Some Multivariate Models and Their Implications, *Journal of Information Technology*, 12, 15-32.

Csikszentmihalyi M. (1990), *Flow: The Psychology of Optimal Experience*, New York, Harper and Row.

Deshpande R. (1983), Paradigm Lost: On Theory and Method in Research in Marketing, *Journal of Marketing*, 47, (fall), 101-109.

Dickerson M. D. et Gentry J. W. (1983), Characteristics of Adopters and Non-adopters of Home Computers, *Journal of Consumer Research*, 10, september, 225-235.

Ellis S. R. (1994), What Are Virtual Environments? *Computer Graphics and Application*, 14, 1, pp. 532-550.

Emmanouilides C. et Hammond K. (2000), Internet Usage: Predictors of Active Users and Frequency of Use, *Journal of Interactive Marketing*, 14, 2, 17-32.

Eveno E. et d'Iribarne A. (1997), Les utilisateurs comme co-concepteurs de services multimédia interactifs: le projet "Ville numérisée" à Parthenay, *Penser les usages, Colloque international*, 1997.

Fromklin H. L. (1971), A Social Psychological Analysis of the Adoption and Diffusion of New Products and Practices from a Uniqueness Motivation Perspective, *Advances in Consumer Research*, Gardner D. M. ed., 2, 464-469.

Galan J-P et Vernette E. (2000), Vers une 4ème Génération: les études de marché on-line, *Décision Marketing*, 19, Janvier/Avril, 39-51.

Gatignon H. et Robertson T. S. (1985), Propositional Inventory for New Diffusion Research, *Journal of Consumer Research*, 11, 849-867.

Hanson W. (2000), *Principles of Internet Marketing*, South-Western College Publishing.

Hert P. (1999), Internet comme dispositif hétérotopique, *Hermes*, 25, 93-107.

Hoffman D. L. et Novak T. P. (1996a), Marketing in Hypermedia Computer-Mediated Environments: Conceptual Foundations, *Journal of Marketing*, 60, July, 60-68.

Hoffman D. L. et Novak T. P. (1996b), A New Paradigm for Electronic Commerce, Working paper, Owen Graduate School of Management, Vanderbilt University: Internet ref: *http://www.2000.ogsm.vanderbilt.edu/novak/new.marketing.paradigm.html*

Holbrook M. B. (1994), The Nature of Customer Value, in *Service Quality: New Directions in Theory and Practice*, R. T. Rust et R. L Olivier Eds., Thousand Oaks: Sage Publications, 21-71.

Jones S. (1999), *Doing Internet Research: Critical Issues and Methods for Examining the Net*, Sage Publications.

Jouet J. (1993), Usages et pratiques des nouveaux outils de communication, *Dictionnaire critique de la communication*, sous la direction de L. Sfez, Paris: PUF.

Kerschner P. A. et Chelsvig K. A. (1981), The Aged User and Technology, *Conference on Communications Technology and the Elderly: Issues and Forecasts*, October 22-23, Cleveland, Ohio.

Lauria R. (1997), Virtual Reality: An Empirical-Metaphysical Testbed, *Journal of Computer Mediated Communication*, Internet ref: *http://www.ascusc.org/jcmc/vol3/issue2/lauria.html*

Lescher J. F. (1995), *On Line Market Research*, Addison-Wesley Publishing Company.

Levy P. (1997), *L'intelligence collective. Pour une anthropologie du cyberespace*, La découverte. Poche.

Levy P. (1998), L'universel sans totalité: essence de la Cyberculture, *Sociétés*, 59, Janvier, 20-30.

Millerand F. (1999), Usages des NTIC: les approches de la diffusion, de l'innovation et de l'appropriation, 2ème partie, *Commposite*, *http://commposite.uqam.ca/99.1/articles/ntic_2.htm*

McCracken G. (1988), *The Long Interview*, Newbury Park (CA), Sage.

Mitchell W. J. (1998), Villes numériques, *Sociétés*, 59, Janvier, 33-40.

Nicovitch S. et Cornwell T. B. (1999), An Internet Culture? Implication for Marketing, *Journal of Interactive Marketing*, 12, 4, 22-33.

Peterson R. A., Balasubramanian S. et Bronnenberg B. J. (1997), Marketing in the 21st Century: Exploring the Implication of the Internet for Consumer Marketing, *Journal of Academy of Marketing Science*, 25, 2, 329-346.

Price L., Arnould J. et Curasi C. F. (2000), Older Consumer's Disposition of Special Possessions, *Journal of Consumer Research*, 27, Septembre, 179-201.

Prust R. C. (1987), Generic Social Processes: Maximizing Conceptual Development in Ethnographic Research, *Journal of Contemporary Ethnography*, 16, 250-293.

Ram S. (1987), A Model of Innovation Resistance, Advances in Consumer Research, 14, Wallendof M. et Anderson P. ed., Provo (UT), *Association for Consumer Research*, 208-212.

Roehrich G. (1994), Innovativités Hédoniste et sociale: proposition d'une échelle de mesure, *Recherche et Application en Marketing*, 9, 2, 19-42.

Rosen L. D. et Weil M. M. (1995), Adult and Teenage Use of Consumer, Business, and Entertainment Technology: Potholes on the Information Superhighway? *Journal of Consumer Affairs*, 29, 1, 55-69.

Rosen L. D., Sears D. C. et Weil M. M. (1987), Computer Phobia, *Behavior Research Methods, Instruments, and Computers*, 19, 167-179.

Rosnay (de) J. (1995), *L'homme symbiotique*, Editions du Seuil (Points).

Serres M. (1997), La rédemption du savoir: des autoroutes pour tous, Propos recueuillis par L. Join-Lambert et P.Klein, *Revue Quart Monde*, 163, (mars).

Sterne J. (1995), *World Wide Web Marketing: Integrating the Internet into your Marketing Strategy*, New York: John Wiley and Sons.

Steuer J. (1992), Defining virtual reality: Dimensions determining telepresence, *Journal of Communication*, 42, 4, 73-93.

Tamaro-Hans A. (1999), Les incidences du Passage: Activité/Retraite sur le consommateur, *Décisions Marketing*, 18, Septembre, 61-67.

Watzlawick P. (1980), *Le langage du changement*, Editiuon du seuil, Paris.

Michelle Bergadaà and Mohamed Jamil Hebali 69

Wittezaele J.-J. et Garcia T. (1992), *A la recherche de l'Ecole de Palo Alto*, Edition du Seuil, Paris: 1992.
Wolcott H. F. (1990), *Writing Up Qualitative Research*, Newbury Park, CA: Sage.
Zeithaml V. A. et Gilly M. C. (1987), Characteristics Affecting the Acceptance of Retailing Technologies: A Comparison of Eldery and Nonelderly Consumers, *Journal of Retailing*, 63, 1, 49-68.

APPENDIX 1
On-Line Opened Questionnaire

1. How did you discover Internet?
2. Why do you use mainly Internet?
3. Do you think that Internet is a social revolution?
4. Personally, what do you think of Internet?
5. What do you like and what attracts you in Internet?
6. What makes you displeased and restraints you in Internet?
7. How did you learn how to use the computer and Internet?
8. In your opinion, has Internet changed your life?
9. On average, how many hours per week do you use Internet?

Confidential questions:

10. Your age:
11. Year of your possible retirement:
12. Your ex-profession:
13. Your home country:

Interpersonal Communication and Personal Influence on the Internet: A Framework for Examining Online Word-of-Mouth

Pamela Kiecker
Deborah Cowles

SUMMARY. This paper reports a preliminary investigation into interpersonal communication and personal influence on the Internet. It addresses the potential need to reformulate current thinking about what comprises interpersonal communication to address its specific use in an interactive electronic environment. We look particularly at one of the most potent forms of interpersonal communication–word-of-mouth (WOM)–and offer a typology for examining online WOM. A review of current online activities uncovers ways in which both consumers and businesses are using WOM, which represent tactics heretofore unavailable via traditional media. Findings suggest the need to expand our view of interpersonal communication and personal influence to include special cases of online sources and online WOM. *[Article copies available for a fee from The Haworth Document Delivery Service: 1-800-HAWORTH. E-mail address: <getinfo@haworthpressinc.com> Website: <http://www.HaworthPress.com> © 2001 by The Haworth Press, Inc. All rights reserved.]*

Pamela Kiecker and Deborah Cowles are affiliated with Virginia Commonwealth University.

[Haworth co-indexing entry note]: "Interpersonal Communication and Personal Influence on the Internet: A Framework for Examining Online Word-of-Mouth." Kiecker, Pamela, and Deborah Cowles. Co-published simultaneously in *Journal of Euromarketing* (International Business Press, an imprint of The Haworth Press, Inc.) Vol. 11, No. 2, 2001, pp. 71-88; and: *Internet Applications in Euromarketing* (ed: Lynn R. Kahle) International Business Press, an imprint of The Haworth Press, Inc., 2001, pp. 71-88. Single or multiple copies of this article are available for a fee from The Haworth Document Delivery Service [1-800-HAWORTH, 9:00 a.m. - 5:00 p.m. (EST). E-mail address: getinfo@haworthpressinc.com].

71

KEYWORDS. Interpersonal communication, personal influence, word-of-mouth, Internet

INTRODUCTION

A recent cartoon showed a dog at a computer in dialogue with a human via the Internet. The cartoon's caption read: "On the Internet, nobody knows you're a dog!" The cartoon's underlying message is an important one. The unique nature of the Internet as a communications medium makes it possible for buyers and sellers operating in the online world to do and say, as well as *become*, virtually anything. And, not unlike the dog in the cartoon, there are examples of how individuals and organizations alike have used this fact to their advantage.

Among the myriad marketing implications of the Internet–a widely accessible one-to-one interactive communications medium–is its impact on the phenomenon known as word-of-mouth (WOM) communication. WOM has been defined as face-to-face (or person-to-person) verbal communication (e.g., exchanges of comments, thoughts, or ideas) between two or more consumers, none of whom represents a marketing source (Bone 1995). While the role of WOM in the marketing communications mix is well-established, no research to date has examined the phenomenon on the Internet where interpersonal communication processes can be viewed as among the most powerful influence mechanisms in our society today.

At almost any time, any Internet user is capable of reaching one to an unlimited number of other Internet users in a manner that could be perceived as personal. The explosiveness of this phenomenon can be observed in the thousands of Internet newsgroups that articulate product praises and consumer complaints, seek information, report personal experiences, and ask for or offer assistance (Stauss 1997). Similarly, in another prevalent form of interpersonal communication via the Internet, online chat forums are used by consumers to "talk" to one another via their respective keyboards. These chat rooms are rapidly becoming a well-established venue for personal influence in the marketplace. The significant role the Internet plays in enhancing the power of individual consumers' messages is also evidenced in the rise of online or "virtual" communities growing up around almost every imaginable consumer activity and interest.

This paper examines WOM communication on the Internet. As background, we first provide a brief summary of traditional WOM communication, especially its role as a type of *personal influence*. We identify five traditional sources of interpersonal influence and describe the role that source *credibility* plays in the effectiveness (acceptance and use) of WOM. We then offer a new typology for understanding WOM on the Internet, describing four distinct categories of online WOM. These two frameworks are used to discuss findings from a review of current online activities of consumers and businesses, providing exemplars of the different types of online WOM as exercised by different sources, exploring different credibility characteristics. Findings suggest the need to expand our current models of interpersonal communication and personal influence to reflect the opportunities and challenges presented by the online environment.

INTERPERSONAL COMMUNICATION AND PERSONAL INFLUENCE

Findings from decades of research on traditional (i.e., off-line) shopping and purchase behavior have shown that consumers are influenced by those with whom they interact. Research has consistently demonstrated that personal sources of information have a strong impact on consumer preferences and choices (Arndt 1967; King and Summers 1970; Herr, Kardes, and Kim 1991). Studies examining purchases of both durable and non-durable consumer goods reveal a significant percentage of consumers rely on personal sources of information when they make product purchases–up to 90% of respondents in one study of major durables (Price and Feick 1984). Consumers contemplating the purchase of services or making decisions involving social and/or financial risks show a pronounced preference for personal sources of information (Beatty and Smith 1987; Formisano, Olshavsky, and Tapp 1982; Murray 1991). In the most general terms, this phenomenon is known as *personal influence*. Personal influence refers to any change, whether deliberate or inadvertent, in an individual's beliefs, attitudes, and/or behaviors, that occurs as the consequence of interpersonal communications (Hanna and Wozniak 2001).

One of the most powerful categories of personal influence in the marketplace is WOM. WOM is person-to-person communication between a receiver and a source that the receiver perceives as noncommercial (Day 1971). The power of WOM to motivate attitudes and behaviors is well accepted in both academic and practitioner realms. For example, estimates regarding negative WOM suggest that almost 60% of dissatisfied consumers tell at least one friend or acquaintance about the dissatisfying experience (Richins 1983). People generally think about WOM in terms of advice given and received within the context of face-to-face conversations. In reality, WOM communication can be transmitted in a variety of ways including in person, over the phone, through the mail and, with increasing frequency, via the Internet. In any setting, the influence of WOM communications cannot be separated from the communicator or source. Therefore, as further background for understanding personal influence via the Internet, we now turn to an examination of WOM sources and the related issue of source credibility.

Personal Sources and Source Credibility

Different sources of personal influence via WOM are commonly recognized in the literature. For example, a vast amount of WOM is communicated and received by individuals who could be considered "typical consumers," often relaying situational information (e.g., a late delivery of a package, a particularly helpful retail salesperson, a seemingly deceptive advertisement). However, the literature also recognizes formal categories of personal influence, each of which performs a somewhat unique role or operates in a particular context relative to the consumer. While WOM communication by "typical consumers" that enters into everyday conversations in a less-than-formal way is by no means insignificant in the marketplace, we focus here on the established categories of personal influence and WOM. We believe this focus provides greater insight and opportunity in an interactive electronic business environment.

When confronting unusual circumstances, unfamiliar issues, and/or challenging decisions, individuals in search of pertinent information frequently turn to others within their social sphere that are better informed on the subject. These more knowledgeable people who provide product-specific advice are known as *opinion leaders*. Opinion leaders are influential with consumers as sources of information and advice because of their involvement, expertise, and experience in a product category (Myers and Robertson 1972; King and Summers 1970; Richins and Root-Shaffer 1998; Venkatraman 1990).

Another source of personal influence is *market mavens*. Market mavens are distinguishable from opinion leaders because their influence stems not from product category expertise, but from general knowledge or market expertise. Market mavens possess a wide range of information about many different types of products, retail outlets, and other aspects of markets. They share information because of their interest in others' welfare (i.e., for altruistic reasons). Market mavens like to browse and shop, and they like to talk about what they observe and learn (Feick and Price 1987; Slama and Williams 1990).

A third influential personal source is *purchase pals*. Purchase pals are individuals who accompany shoppers to the point of purchase and act as a source of information and/or social support and thereby influence shoppers during the actual shopping trip (Kiecker and Hartman 1995, 1994, 1993; Hartman and Kiecker 1994, 1991). While purchase pals also may be opinion leaders or market mavens, their unique influence is tied to the role they play at the point of purchase. For example, Kiecker and Hartman (1993, 1994) show that purchase pals often are responsible for actual product selection and negotiation of final purchase prices. Their research also has shown that consumers select different purchase pals for different shopping objectives, including social as well as functional or task-specific ones.

Innovators or early adopters of new products represent another type of influential personal source due to their experience with *new products*. They can exert either a passive or active influence on later purchasers. For highly-visible projects (e.g., automobiles), much information is transmitted from early to later purchasers simply by product use. Research has indicated that early adopters will talk about products and that there is, indeed, a group of influential early adopters. Like opinion leaders, research suggests that early adopters are product-specific (Baumgarten 1975; Robertson 1971).

A fifth formally-recognized personal source is the *surrogate consumer*. A surrogate consumer is "an agent retained by a consumer to guide, direct, or transact marketplace activities" (Solomon 1986). Unlike other personal sources, the surrogate is usually financially compensated for this involvement. Surrogates are used by consumers who may lack the know-how, time, or desire to personally search for information, evaluate alternatives, and make choices. Consequently, they employ an intermediary for these purposes. While many surrogate consumers are "independents," others may be commissioned employees of business organizations, which likely influences the recommendations they provide consumers and the choices they make on behalf of consumers. By definition, since they are paid for their services, surrogates do not engage in what is technically WOM. However, we feel they provide WOM-like communication, as the messages communicated are often seen as originating from a source more independent of the marketer when compared to a salesperson or other paid employees. Indeed, the effectiveness of a surrogate consumer's WOM likely would be related closely to the extent to which consumers believed the information provided was independent of marketer influence.

A primary determinant of the influence of the information communicated is the perceived credibility of the source of the information. *Source credibility* is the extent to which the receiver (1) sees the source as having relevant knowledge, skill, or experience and (2) trusts the source to give unbiased, objective information (Belch and Belch 2001). As suggested by this definition, credibility has two dimensions–expertise and trustworthiness. Characteristics such as knowledge, intelligence, maturity, and professional or social status all lend an air of expertise to individuals. A source with expertise is more persuasive than one with less expertise. But the source also has to be trustworthy. Although many definitions of trust have been provided in the marketing literature (e.g., Doney and Cannon 1997; Moorman, Deshpande, and Zaltman 1993; Morgan and Hunt 1994), we feel the dimensions of trust most critical to WOM are (1) the influencer is motivated by the best interests of the individual receiving the message and, related to the first dimension, (2) the influencer will not take advantage of any vulnerability on the part of the receiver. Research has shown that the influence of a personal source will be less if the receiver thinks the source is biased or has underlying personal motives for his or her recommendation (O'Keefe 1987).

Another source attribute contributing to perceived credibility is *attractiveness*. It encompasses similarity, familiarity, and likability (Triandis 1971) and reflects the extent to which the receiver identifies with the source. Similarity is a supposed resemblance between the source and the receiver. Research suggests that the more receivers feel that a source is similar to themselves (or how they would like to think of themselves), the more likely they will perceive the source as credible and, therefore, be persuaded (Chaiken 1979; Kahle and Homer 1985). Familiarity refers to knowledge of the source through exposure or past association whereby a level of comfort with the source is established for the receiver. Likability is an affection for the source as a result of physical appearance, behavior, or other personal traits (talent, personality, etc.). Both familiarity and likability influence positively the extent to which the consumer perceives the source to have the consumer's best interests in mind. Research has shown that the greater the perceived attractiveness of the source–a function of similarity, familiarity, and likability–the more persuasive the communication. While the credibility of opinion leaders has been found to derive primarily from their knowledge and perceived expertise, they (as well as other personal sources) may derive credibility from perceived trustworthiness, similarity, familiarity, and/or likability (Myers and Robertson, 1972). Therefore, in our investigation of online influencers, each of these attributes will be examined to determine the extent to which personal sources–including those developed for commercial use by businesses–use such characteristics to establish credibility online, and how consumers perceive and interpret the same credibility cues online.

Figure 1 represents the foregoing discussion. It defines five "formal" sources of WOM communication and summarizes the characteristics that influence their perceived credibility. As indicated in Figure 1, *Opinion Leaders* are more likely to derive their credibility from expertise and trustworthiness than from attractiveness. Opinion Leaders influence consumers' brand choices within product categories by providing WOM recommendations that are viewed as credible due to their involvement, expertise, and experience in a product category and the receiver's belief (trust) that the Opinion Leader has no vested interest in nor anything to gain personally from their purchase. *Market Mavens* are viewed similarly. However, as shown in Figure 1, they are noted for their expertise in the general marketplace (i.e., the quantity

FIGURE 1. Sources of WOM Communications and Their Credibility Characteristics

PERSONAL SOURCES	Expertise	Trustworthiness	Attractiveness Similarity, Familiarity, and Likability
1. Opinion Leaders Provide product specific advice based on their involvement, expertise, and experience in a product category.	YES Product Category	YES	VARIES
2. Market Mavens Possess a wide range of information about many different types of products, retail outlets, and other aspects of markets that they share with others.	YES General Marketplace	YES	VARIES
3. Purchase Pals Accompany shoppers to the point of purchase to assist in decision-making during the actual shopping trip.	VARIES	YES	VARIES
4. Innovators/Early Adopters Talk to others about their experience with new products.	YES Product Category	YES	VARIES
5. Surrogate Consumers Guide, direct, or transact marketplace activities on behalf of consumers for a fee.	YES	VARIES	VARIES

and quality of information they possess about a wide range of products, retail stores, etc.) rather than expertise in a specific product category. Not unlike Opinion Leaders, Market Mavens are perceived to be trustworthy due to their altruistic motives. Further, they do not stand to gain from a consumer's particular choice of a product or distributor. *Purchase Pals* have been shown to derive their credibility from trustworthiness more than any other credibility characteristic. While Purchase Pals may or may not be perceived as expert, consumers rely on their WOM communication to be honest, objective, and free of bias. *Innovators and Early Adopters* of products are influential sources of WOM communication due to both expertise and trustworthiness. Their expertise stems from their direct experience with new products, while their trustworthiness stems from their status as an "average consumer" without any ties or affiliation with the marketer of the new product. *Surrogate consumers*, while viewed as credible sources of WOM communication due to their expertise, may or may not be viewed as trustworthy due to two important defining characteristics of their role as a WOM source. The first is the fact that they receive payment for their activities–for guiding, directing, or making purchases on behalf of consumers. The second is their explicit or implied relationship with the businesses whose goods and services they represent. As shown in Figure 1, the credibility characteristic of attractiveness (including similarity, familiarity, and likability) varies across all five sources of WOM communication. Accordingly, attractiveness can be viewed as a less defining characteristic of the credibility of WOM sources than both expertise and trustworthiness.

A TYPOLOGY OF ONLINE WOM COMMUNICATIONS

Our investigation into online WOM involved a review of current online activities of both consumers and businesses. Our review included (1) examination of popular press and online media vehicles focusing on reports of consumers' online activities and current practices of online businesses and (2) visits to more than 100 Web sites. It revealed many forms of WOM in the Internet environment. As an initial framework for classifying the many forms, we suggest four distinct categories (see Figure 2). We label the first category *spontaneous* WOM. This type of online WOM is initiated and/or carried out by individual consumers using their own means and know-how (e.g., via a personal e-mail account or personal homepage). *Spontaneous* WOM is the online form of WOM

FIGURE 2. Word-of-Mouth Communication in an Internet Environment

Types of Online WOM	Definitions	Examples of Positive Communications	Examples of Negative Communications
1. Spontaneous	Initiated and/or carried out by individual consumers using their own means and know how (e.g., via a personal email account or homepage).	A consumer sends an email message to friends and family members in her personal address book telling everyone about a great movie she saw; a consumer prepares a personal review of a local restaurant and emails it to friends he thinks may also enjoy the restaurant.	A consumer sends an email message to friends and family members in his or her personal address book telling everyone about a really bad book or bad movie, or a lousy experience at a new restaurant (bad food, poor service).
2. Quasi-Spontaneous	Initiated and/or carried out by individual consumers in web environments created by marketers (e.g., corporate Web sites).	A consumer posts a positive book review at Amazon.com; a user provides a high rating of a vendor on eBay.	A consumer posts a negative book review at Amazon.com; a user provides a cautionary comment regarding a seemingly unscrupulous dealer on eBay.
3. Independent- or Third Party-sponsored	Initiated and/or carried out by individual consumers in web environments created by special interest groups, professional associations, and/or organizations for purposes other than selling products.	A consumer tells other women about a great new drug for PMS through the online community at iVillage.com; a kit car enthusiast provides a recommendation of a particular company's products and services based on his recent order on Kitcar.com.	A woman uses iVillage.com's chat room to warn other mothers about a company that seems to be targeting children with an online scam; a kit car enthusiast uses Kitcar.com to report the failed delivery of a kit purchased via an online dealer and warns others against using said dealer.
4. Corporate-Sponsored	Initiated by marketers, but carried out by individual consumers who are paid and/or otherwise motivated to "spread the word" about a product or company for the purposes of selling its products or promoting the company.	A company pays consumers to monitor activity in its chat rooms and to participate in discussions in a way that ensures other consumers will hear consistently good messages about their products; the company uses its paid consumer advisors to post positive comments, reviews, and ratings of its products among user groups.	A company pays consumers to participate in user groups, chat rooms, and/or online communities of its competitors and through this participation, to offer negative reviews, evaluations, misinformation, or to start and/or encourage negative rumors about other businesses or market factors that may affect the company and its products; the company uses its paid consumer advisors to steer users away from competitors' products by emphasizing bad product features in their product comparisons.

that is most like informal WOM in traditional marketing settings. Individual consumers can be proactive in terms of offering WOM via the Internet. An example of such was provided in a *60 Minutes' report of a 16-year-old stock investor who made glowing predictions for penny stocks via the Internet by sending hundreds of personal e-mail messages via different e-mail accounts/names and was credited with influencing others' investments and thereby manipulating the market for his personal gain ("Pump and Dump," CBS News Broadcast*, Sunday, October 22, 2000). Spontaneous WOM also can be reactive in terms of responding to information from other consumers. The "reply" function (which generally offers a "reply to all" option) that is customary in e-mail services attests to the fact that responding to information from others is a common online consumer behavior. Unlike most traditional WOM, it is important to note that sources of *spontaneous* WOM may or may not be strongly tied to the individuals exposed to their messages (i.e., they may or may not be close friends or family members, co-workers or neighbors). It is the ability of *spontaneous* WOM communicators to reach such a vast audience of consumers via the Internet with very little cost or effort that sets this category of WOM apart from its traditional counterpart.

The second category of online WOM includes consumers who participate in what we label *quasi-spontaneous* WOM. It is initiated and/or carried out by individual consumers, but in environments created or encouraged by marketers. Examples of *quasi-spontaneous* WOM include book and music reviews written by consumers at corporate Web sites such as *Amazon.com* and participation in company-hosted electronic chat rooms or bulletin boards such as those provided for buyers and sellers at eBay. By chatting at the eBay Café or through the bulletin boards, users petition one another for information about specific products they are interested in buying or selling, as well as prior experience with vendors. To a greater extent than *spontaneous* WOM, sources of *quasi-spontaneous* WOM are unfamiliar with the individuals exposed to their messages (i.e., they are not close friends or family members, co-workers or neighbors, but rather unacquainted strangers, for all intents and purposes). For these reasons, we believe that *quasi-spontaneous* WOM is unlike both *spontaneous* online WOM and traditional WOM communication.

A third category of online WOM is *independent- or third party-sponsored*. It is initiated and/or carried out by individuals in environments created by special interest groups, professional associations, and/or organizations for purposes other than selling products. Instead of selling products, these sites represent a wide variety of perspectives on different categories of goods and services as well as a variety of topics such as hobbies, interests, and activities. One example of such a site is *AskJeeves.com*, which is designed to supply consumers with fast access to answers to a wide variety of questions. Users pose questions in their own words and receive links to Web sites containing relevant information on goods and services based on millions of previous searches conducted for other users. Ask Jeeves includes an "Ask the Experts" option that allows users to seek the counsel of self-designated experts who have been rated on the basis of their performance as advisors by previous users. Another example of *independent or third party-sponsored* WOM is evidenced at *Epinions.com*, which claims to offer over one million reviews by and comments of consumers and to cover over 200,000 goods and services to help users make better buying decisions. *Epinions.com* includes a "Web of Trust" feature that it claims "mimics the way people share word-of-mouth advice every day." Users' involvement in building their "Web of Trust" on the site helps the *Epinions.com* system decide automatically how useful an opinion, service, or good may be to specific users.

A fourth and final category of online WOM is *corporate-sponsored.* Based on our traditional definitions of WOM, *corporate-sponsored* WOM technically is not WOM communication at all due to the commercial nature of the source of the message. However, because it has the capability of being *perceived* as WOM by consumers, we believe it needs to be addressed as such. *Corporate-sponsored* WOM is initiated by marketers, but carried out by individual consumers who are paid and/or other motivated to "spread the word" about a product or company for the purposes of selling its products or promoting the company. *Corporate-sponsored* WOM has emerged, we contend, because marketers understand the power of WOM communication, especially as they struggle to differentiate and position themselves in cyberspace. This category of online WOM reflects at least two different online tactics. The first is the use of company employees to monitor lists and newsgroups that discuss their products and those of their competitors with the goal of managing the quality and quantity of information shared within online environments. As a result of such monitoring, they can quickly detect emerging problems and respond to statements that may be incorrect. In the same way, less scrupulous businesses can actually spread negative information to adversely impact competitors' standings. For many businesses, "eavesdropping" on customers' online conversations is an important source of market intelligence and is becoming an element of their public relations programs. Another type of "monitoring" in this corporate-sponsored environment is exemplified by a relatively new service, Icontact, offered by *Heyinc.com*. The service tracks consumers' movements through web sites, and customer service representatives step in if they believe they are needed. A second online tactic that represents *corporate-sponsored* WOM is featuring individual experts or *personae* (real or simulated) whose scripted role is to recommend goods and services to consumers visiting the corporate Web site. One example is the Meeting Place at *MarthaStewart.com* where shoppers can "talk" with Martha and other experts about goods and services, as well as activities and interests represented on the site. While it is not the case for all *corporate-sponsored* WOM scenarios, one can imagine cases where such WOM communicators could be likened to the dog at the PC in the opening scenario, except the caption would read, "On the Internet, no one knows I'm really a paid employee." Examples in Figure 2 show how both positive and negative communications are possible within each of the four categories of online WOM.

INTEGRATING THE FRAMEWORKS

Using the two frameworks presented in Figure 1 and Figure 2 above, the focus of our exploratory investigation was to identify prototypes of the five categories of personal influence in the online environment. This section discusses our findings.

As indicated in a previous section of this paper, although *spontaneous* WOM is perhaps most like traditional WOM communication, the unique capabilities of the Internet demand that it be considered separately. While e-mail messages between and among Internet users who know each other personally would be very similar to traditional WOM, the fact that e-mail is forwarded so easily with little time cost and virtually no monetary cost, it is clear that *spontaneous* WOM has much greater reach than traditional WOM. Another distinction between *spontaneous* WOM and traditional WOM is the fact that sources have many more options available in terms of communicating information about a product or a company. One example is the near legendary *Untied* Airlines Web site (*www.Untied.com*). It began as one consumer's dissatisfaction with service provided by United Airlines. Today, it provides a highly systematic process for the wide dissemination of negative information about United Airlines, with buttons on the homepage including

Rudeness, *Misinformation*, *Incompetence*, and *Refund Problems*. Similarly, the widely disseminated Neiman Marcus chocolate cookie recipe
represents the power of viral marketing (*www.urbandlegends.com/ulz/
twofifty.html*; Harmon 2001). The false story of a woman forced to pay
$250 for the cookie recipe spread from each message recipient to hun-
dreds of others with each request to "share the message." While we encourage marketers to recognize that *spontaneous* WOM is different
from traditional WOM in the ways outlined above (and we call for additional research to determine the cues used by consumers to assess the
credibility of *spontaneous* WOM from various sources), the subsequent
discussion is focused on the remaining three types of online WOM that
directly or indirectly involve commercial sources of communication. It
is these types of online WOM that we believe represent the greatest
break from our traditional understanding of WOM.

Turning to the other three forms of online WOM communication,
(1) *quasi-spontaneous*, (2) *independent- or third-party*, and (3) *corporate-sponsored*, we offer Figure 3 as a means of integrating the personal
source (Figure 1) and online WOM type (Figure 2) frameworks. Figure
3 also includes examples of how source credibility manifests itself in
various online WOM venues. Each case poses a particular challenge in-
asmuch as it may be more difficult for (potentially vulnerable) users to
assess the traditional cues used to determine credibility and easier for
businesses and other vested sources to manipulate/simulate credibility
characteristics to their commercial advantage. Importantly, further research is needed to determine (1) the extent to which each of the five
personal source roles is effective in *quasi-spontaneous*, *independent- or
third-party*, and/or *corporate-sponsored* WOM settings, and (2) how
each of the characteristics of credibility can be manipulated to enhance
the impact of the communicated message.

It should be noted that although none of the examples included in
Figure 3 is negative, it is at least conceivable that negative communication could take place in these settings. In particular, in each of the examples of online WOM offered, it is not uncommon for negative product
information to be communicated in such venues. Although it is far less
likely that negative information would find its way into *corporate-sponsored* WOM, it appears as though some companies attempt to
manipulate perceived credibility by providing information about competitors' offerings, which at times influences the consumer to purchase
a competing product.

Due to the ability to "be anything" on the Internet, it is quite possible
that consumers receiving online WOM communications could be un-

FIGURE 3. Manipulations of Personal Sources and Credibility Characteristics in Online WOM

TYPE OF ONLINE WOM	EXEMPLAR MANIPULATIONS OF PERSONAL SOURCES	EXEMPLAR MANIPULATIONS OF CREDIBILITY CHARACTERISTICS
1. **Quasi-Spontaneous** Initiated and/or carried out by individual consumers in web environments created by marketers (e.g., corporate Web sites)	**1. Opinion Leaders** Product evaluations are provided by self-designated experts at Epinions.com. **2. Purchase Pals** Shoppers are allowed to browse the site together and may even add items to a shared shopping cart on Landsend.com's "shop with a friend" option. **3. Innovators/Early Adopters** Early adopters of books and music provide reviews and ratings of the books and music for other consumers to consider.	1. **Expertise** is indicated by information about individual's background (credentials) and prior experience with the product. 2. **Attractiveness** is engendered by allowing consumers to share the online shopping task with friends/family members who are similar, familiar, and/or likable. 3. **Trustworthiness** results from the perceived objectivity of "real people" serving as reviewers; **Attractiveness** is engendered due to perceived similarity between shoppers and recommenders.
2. **Independent or Third Party-Sponsored** Initiated and/or carried out by individual consumers in web environments created by special interest groups, professional associations, and/or organizations for purposes other than selling products.	**1. Opinion Leaders** AskJeeves.com provides access to a variety of "experts" who provide answers to users' questions. **2. Market Mavens** Unbiased information about a wide range of different online products and providers is available to consumers at mysimon.com. **3. Surrogate Consumers** Input to consumer decision making is provided by other consumers who charge by the minute for their responses to users' questions on keen.com.	1. **Expertise** is established by the profiles of experts provided on the site. 2. **Trustworthiness** results from the fact that the site provides objective information about a variety of competing products and businesses. 3. **Attractiveness** (similarity) is engendered by virtue of the "real person" status of the surrogate consumer.
3. **Corporate-Sponsored** Initiated by marketers, but carried out by "individuals" who are paid and/or otherwise motivated to "spread the word" about a product or company for the purposes of selling its products or promoting the company.	**1. Purchase Pals** A company sales representative co-navigates the corporate Web site with the customer or prospect via a shared browser at Hipbone.com.	1. **Expertise** is assumed by virtue of the sales representatives training and experience with the company's goods and services; **Trustworthiness** is conveyed through the "team-based" browsing with the customer/prospect.

aware of the source of the communication. In addition, we believe it is possible for sources to manipulate credibility cues in such a way to motivate consumers to interpret online WOM very differently than traditional WOM communication where credibility characteristics are more concrete and easily verified. Readers are encouraged to think about the wide range of possibilities and consider the implications for a new and expanded understanding of WOM that includes the many possibilities for online WOM.

CONCLUSIONS AND DIRECTIONS FOR FUTURE RESEARCH

It seems clear that the Internet is ushering in an era where the role of personal influence will attain unprecedented prominence (Miller 1999). And, as argued here, WOM does not adequately describe the situation when a single electronic message can reach hundreds of thousands of people in a matter of minutes. This latter fact is further complicated by the ability of consumers and businesses alike to manipulate the cues that have traditionally been used by both to assess the credibility of and ascribe credibility to different information sources in ways heretofore unavailable via traditional media.

While we previously viewed personal influence as something that occurs when strong social ties exist between information receivers and senders (Brown and Reingen 1987), such is not the case for online WOM. Due to the Internet, interpersonal communication is no longer restricted to the small circle of family and friends that personal sources were assumed to have, wherein source credibility was quite obvious and rarely suspect.

It is our contention that establishing credibility is essential in a setting such as the Internet, where business success increasingly will be determined by the extent to which consumers can trust the individuals and companies with which they interact. A better understanding of the determinants of source credibility in online interpersonal settings is needed to guide marketing strategies and tactics for the new media into the future. The background and initial framework for investigating online WOM developed here should serve as a foundation for future examinations of the specific nature of interpersonal communication and personal influence on the Internet.

REFERENCES

Arndt, Johan (1967), "Role of Product-Related Conversations in the Diffusion of a New Product," *Journal of Marketing Research* 4 (August), 291-295.

Baumgarten, Steven A. (1975), "The Innovative Communicator in the Diffusion Process," *Journal of Marketing Research* 12 (February), 12-18.

Belch and Belch (2001). *Advertising and Promotion: An Integrated Marketing Communications Perspective, 5th edition*, (Irwin McGraw-Hill).

Beatty, Sharon E. and Scott M. Smith (1987), "External Search Efforts: An Investigation Across Several Product Categories," *Journal of Consumer Research*, 14 (June), 83-95.

Bone, Paula Fitzgerald (1995), "Word-of-Mouth Effects on Short-Term and Long-Term Product Judgments," *Journal of Business Research*, 32 (2), 213-223.

Brown, Jacqueline Johnson and Peter H. Reingen (1987), "Social Ties and Word-of-Mouth Referral Behavior," *Journal of Consumer Research* 14 (December), 350-362.

Chaiken, Shelly (1979), "Communicator Physical Attractiveness and Persuasion," *Journal of Personality and Social Psychology*, 37 (August), 1387-1397.

Day, George S. (1971), "Attitude Change, Media, and Word-of-Mouth," *Journal of Advertising Research*, 11, No. 6, 31-40.

Doney, P. M. and Joseph P. Cannon (1997), "An Examination of the Nature of Trust in Buyer-Seller Relationships," *Journal of Marketing*, 61 (April), 35-52.

Feick, Lawrence F. and Linda L. Price (1987), "The Market Maven: A Diffuser of Marketplace Information," *Journal of Marketing*, 51 (January), 83-97.

Formisano, Roger A., Richard W. Olshavsky and Shelley Tapp (1982), "Choice Strategy in a Difficult Task Environment," *Journal of Consumer Research*, 8 (March), 474-479.

Hanna, Nessim and Richard Wozniak (2001), *Consumer Behavior: An Applied Approach* (Upper Saddle River, NJ: Prentice Hall).

Harmon, Amy (2001), "The Search for Intelligent Life on the Internet," *New York Times*, September 23.

Hartman, Cathy L. and Pamela L. Kiecker (1991), "Marketplace Influencers at the Point of Purchase: The Role of Purchase Pals in Consumer Decision Making," *Enhancing Knowledge Development in Marketing*, Proceedings of the Summer Educators' Conference (Chicago: American Marketing Association), 461-469.

Hartman, Cathy L. and Pamela Kiecker (1994), "Buyers and Their Purchase Pals: An Examination of This Helping Exchange," *Enhancing Knowledge Development in Marketing*, Proceedings of the Summer Educators' Conference (Chicago: American Marketing Association), 138-144.

Herr, Paul M., Frank R. Kardes and John Kim (1991), "Effects of Word-of-Mouth and Product-Attribute Information on Persuasion: An Accessibility-Diagnosticity Perspective," *Journal of Consumer Research* (March) 17, 454-462.

Kahle, Lynn R. and Pamela M. Homer (1985), "Physical Attractiveness of the Celebrity Endorser: A Social Adaptation Perspective," *Journal of Consumer Research*, 11 (March), 954-961.

Kiecker, Pamela and Cathy L. Hartman (1993), "Purchase Pal Use: Why Buyers Choose to Shop with Others," *Marketing Theory and Applications*, Proceedings of the AMA Winter Educators' Conference (Chicago: American Marketing Association), 378-384.

Kiecker, Pamela and Cathy L. Hartman (1994), "Predicting Buyers' Selection of Interpersonal Sources: The Role of Strong Ties and Weak Ties," *Advances in Consumer Research*, 464-469.

Kiecker, Pamela and Cathy L. Hartman (1995), "Defining the Category of Purchase Pal-Assisted Buyers: Sellers' Declarative and Procedural Knowledge Structures," *Proceedings of the National Conference in Sales Management*, 18-25.

King, Charles W. and John O. Summers (1970), "Overlap of Opinion Leadership Across Consumer Product Categories," *Journal of Marketing Research*, 7, 43-50.

McGuire, William J. (1969), "The Nature of Attitudes and Attitude Change," in *Handbook of Social Psychology*, 2nd ed., eds. G. Lindzey and E. Aronson (Cambridge, Mass.: Addison-Wesley), 135-214.

Miller, Annetta (1999), "The Millennial Mind-Set: It's Here, It's Clear, Get Used to It!", *American Demographics* (January), 60-65.

Moorman, Christine, R. Deshpande, and Gerald Zaltman (1993), "Factors Affecting Trust in Market Research Relationships," *Journal of Marketing*, 15 (January), 81-101.

Morgan, Robert M. and Shelby D. Hunt (1994), "The Commitment-Trust Theory of Relationship Marketing," *Journal of Marketing*, 58 (July), 20-39.

Murray, Keith (1991), "A Test of Services Marketing Theory: Consumer Information Acquisition Activities," *Journal of Marketing*, 55 (January), 10-16.

Myers, James H. and Thomas S. Robertson (1972), "Dimensions of Opinion Leadership," *Journal of Marketing Research*, 9 (February), 41-46.

O'Keefe, Daniel J. (1987), "The Persuasive Effects of Delaying Identification of High- and Low-Credibility Communicators: A Meta-analytic Review," *Central States Speech Journal*, 38, 63-72.

Price, Linda L. and Lawrence F. Feick (1984), "The Role of Interpersonal Sources in External Search: An Informational Perspective," *Advances in Consumer Research*, ed. Thomas C. Kinnear (Ann Arbor, MI: Association for Consumer Research), Vol. 11, 250-253.

Richins, Marsha L. (1983), "Negative Word-of-Mouth by Dissatisfied Consumers: A Pilot Study," *Journal of Marketing*, 47 (Winter), 68-78.

Richins, Marsha and Teri Root-Shaffer (1988), "The Role of Involvement and Opinion Leadership in Consumer Word-of-Mouth: An Implicit Model Made Explicit," in *Advances in Consumer Research*, Michael J. Houston, ed. (Provo, UT: Association for Consumer Research), Vol. 15, 32-36.

Robertson (1971), *Innovative Behavior and Communication* (New York: Holt, Rinehart and Wilson, Inc.).

Slama, Mark E. and Terrell G. Williams (1990), "Generalization of the Market Maven's Information Provision Tendency Across Product Categories," *Advances in Consumer Research*, Thomas K. Srull, ed., Vol. 17, 48-52.

Solomon, Michael R. (1986), "The Missing Link: Surrogate Consumers in the Marketing Chain," *Journal of Marketing* 50 (October), 208-218.

Stauss, Bernd (1997), "Global World-of-Mouth: Service Bashing on the Internet Is a Thorny Issue," *Marketing Management* 6 (Fall), No. 3, 28-30.

Triandis, H.C. (1971), *Attitudes and Attitude Change* (New York: John Wiley & Sons).

Venkatraman, Meera P. (1990), "Opinion Leaders, Adopters, and Communicative Adopters: A Role Analysis," *Psychology and Marketing*, 6 (Spring), 51-68.

Evaluating Negative Information in Online Consumer Discussions: From Qualitative Analysis to Signal Detection

David M. Boush
Lynn Kahle

SUMMARY. Usenet groups, lifestyle portals, professional forums, and other online discussions allow consumers to communicate with each other in unprecedented ways. Negative online word of mouth may pose particular worries for marketing practitioners; but how can marketers tell whether there is a real problem? This paper discusses methods for evaluating negative information in online discussions. Concepts from content analysis and signal detection theory are described and illustrated using two online discussions concerning Nike. *[Article copies available for a fee from The Haworth Document Delivery Service: 1-800-HAWORTH. E-mail address: <getinfo@haworthpressinc.com> Website: <http://www.HaworthPress.com> © 2001 by The Haworth Press, Inc. All rights reserved.]*

KEYWORDS. Internet, information processing, group decisions, word of mouth

David M. Boush and Lynn Kahle are affiliated with the University of Oregon.
Address correspondence to: David M. Boush, University of Oregon, Eugene, OR 97403-1208 USA (E-mail: dmboush@oregon.uoregon.edu).

[Haworth co-indexing entry note]: "Evaluating Negative Information in Online Consumer Discussions: From Qualitative Analysis to Signal Detection." Boush, David M., and Lynn Kahle. Co-published simultaneously in *Journal of Euromarketing* (International Business Press, an imprint of The Haworth Press, Inc.) Vol. 11, No. 2, 2001, pp. 89-105; and: *Internet Applications in Euromarketing* (ed: Lynn R. Kahle) International Business Press, an imprint of The Haworth Press, Inc., 2001, pp. 89-105. Single or multiple copies of this article are available for a fee from The Haworth Document Delivery Service [1-800-HAWORTH, 9:00 a.m. - 5:00 p.m. (EST). E-mail address: getinfo@haworthpressinc.com].

INTRODUCTION

Online Communities

The tremendous growth in computer networks since 1993 has prompted a commensurate increase in interest in online communities. Interactions have become commonplace among people whose social or physical separation previously kept them from communicating. Media such as e-mail, chat, and conferencing systems like Usenet have allowed people to form groups to discuss mutual interests, entertain each other, and work on collective projects. Previous research involving online discussions has focused primarily on the sociology of online communities (Rheingold 1993; Kollock and Smith 1999). Issues such as group hierarchy, gender identity, and online relationships have been in the forefront of such discussions. Online communities have also been assessed in terms of their profit potential (Hagel and Armstrong 1997).

There is yet another purpose of online community with particular relevance for marketers. Marketing practitioners and academics can use these discussions as data to learn about consumers. Consider for example the following posting:

> *I hate Nike straight out. Why? It's not that I hate the name or anything, it is how they treat their workers and how they pay them. They pay their workers 20 cents an hour, and a little under two dollars a day. That is not enough for the workers to buy food! They also abuse the workers. They touch, hit, and make unwanted sexual advances on the women. As women shouldn't we try to do something about this? Please air your views on this company and the other companies that use sweatshops.*

What should Nike make of this? What, exactly, does it indicate about consumer opinion? What action by Nike, if any, is appropriate? The marketing literature has long acknowledged the importance of interpersonal influence as a source of information (Katona and Mueller 1955) including the effect of negative information (Richins 1983; Smith and Vogt 1995). Postings such as the one above represent a new form of word of mouth (WOM), or what Granitz and Ward (1996) call "word on line" (WOL). Bulletin board WOL is not only useful to online interactants, it is potentially useful to those who study them. Online bulletin boards can be a rich source of data describing what consumers all over the world are actually saying to each other, without prompting from marketers.

The purpose of this paper is to describe how online discussion groups, particularly bulletin boards like Usenet, can be treated as a source of consumer data. Our emphasis here will be on negative WOL. First, bulletin board discussions will be treated as a source of qualitative secondary data. Two discussions concerning Nike will be used to illustrate characteristics that may be useful to examine in this context. Next, application of quantitative content analysis will be described. Finally, signal detection theory is discussed as a framework for deciding whether an issue raised in an online discussion should be taken as a serious indicator of consumer discontent.

DISCUSSIONS AS RESEARCH DATA

Various forms of online discussion differ along at least three important dimensions, time, scale, and ability to be archived. E-mail and online bulletin boards provide asynchronous communication, whereas online text chat occurs in real time. As a consequence, chat is probably more spontaneous, like spoken conversation, and a forum is more like mailing a letter. Forum participants can better reflect on and edit their comments as they feel appropriate. The second difference among forms of discussion is scale. E-mail discussions, or listservs, are generally more difficult than bulletin boards to manage on a large scale. That is, the conversation is harder to manage as the number of participants increases. As members of a listserv can attest, too many messages are uninteresting, necessitating some form of hierarchy and control. Because chat occurs in real time, it is also less scalable than bulletin boards. Participants in a chat room have difficulty addressing each other and keeping the discussion focused.

Bulletin boards and other online discussions cannot substitute for more traditional quantitative analysis such as survey research; however, online text discussions provide three advantages over the usual spoken conversation. First, a written text record of online forums exists after the conversation ceases. This text eliminates the need for transcription, which is both effortful and error-prone. Second, online conversations are often extremely accessible. The researcher can get opinions quickly from diverse groups all over the world. Third, bulletin boards, like overheard conversations, provide a window into what people are really saying without contamination from the researcher. As with focus groups, bulletin boards provide a means of learning about how people think about the dimensions of a problem independent of the researcher's cognitive structuring of the issues. Because online discussion exists as written text, it may also be amenable to quantitative content analysis.

In the following section we propose and illustrate some criteria for evaluating online bulletin boards such as Usenet. The criteria may be somewhat different for online text chat and other media; however, many of the same concepts should apply. We also are approaching the online discussions as observers rather than as participants. Certainly much could be learned from posing direct questions to online community members, but this activity would involve an additional set of research issues. Observation and analysis of bulletin boards combines elements of both primary and secondary data collection. The researcher's search for appropriate discussions is active and may be seen as a kind of primary data collection process. Key decisions would involve the target group of interest and the subject key words that identify an interesting discussion; however, discussions online are generated by a question posted by one of the community's members. If the researcher does not engage as a participant, the conversation should be considered as secondary data. Stewart and Kamins (1993) propose that users of secondary data pose questions related to the source of the information and of the information itself. Similarly, content analysis has frequently been guided by examining who said what to whom with what effect (Lasswell 1948).

The same examination of source and message characteristics applies to analysis of online discussions. Since online discussions cast participants as both source and audience, participants may be described in both those roles. Determinants of online data quality concern its context; specifically, the way the discussion is managed, the characteristics of those who take part, and the characteristics of the discussion itself. We should ask the purpose of the discussion and the motivations of participants. We should also question the ability and credibility of participants to discuss a particular subject. As with other secondary analysis we need to examine the units of analysis in an online discussion and find ways to quantify some elements of the conversation. All of the above occurs within the context of a particular discussion community. But first we need to examine the way these communities manage their discussions.

DISCUSSION MANAGEMENT

The discussion to this point suggests that online bulletin boards differ in key respects from both conversations and print media such as newspapers. Like a conversation, participants act as both source and audience for messages. Like print media, online discussions can be edited and leave a physical trace. Online discussions can have rules for participation and management that make them different from both print media and spoken conversation. This affects their analysis for content.

Rules

Communities differ greatly in the rules of participation. The most basic rule governs who participants can be. Some online communities require professional licensing, for example, in a particular health care profession. This requirement enables all participants to trust the information provided. Most online groups are open to all participants and are defined by interest only; however, even when participation is open, some groups actively discourage unwanted members. An example of this discouragement is the hostility expressed toward America Online members in some Usenet discussions, presumably because an aol.com email address indicates ignorance or "newbie" status. Groups can also proscribe certain kinds of behavior, such as shouting (typing in all caps) or flaming (insulting other participants). Generally, stronger membership rules yield stronger communities.

Level of Discussion Management

Communities differ according to how tightly they are managed. More centralized management usually accompanies more stringent rules. For example, discussions among physicians generally require participants to register by e-mail with a discussion administrator, who then issues a password. Usenet bulletin boards have essentially no central administration. One caveat of controlling a discussion is that it tends to imply some responsibility for content. A site that posts messages through some kind of central authority confers an implied acceptability for the postings, much like when a newspaper publishes a letter to the Editor. Therefore, managing a discussion can threaten a company or organization's reputation if it is not done carefully.

As discussed above, characteristics of forum participants are critical in assessing the meaning of online discussions. Participants' contributions depend on both their abilities and their motivations.

DIMENSIONS OF ONLINE DISCUSSIONS

Units of Analysis

In a bulletin board discussion a thread is a more-or-less continuous chain of postings on a single topic. To "follow a thread" is to read a series of postings that share a common subject or (more correctly) that is connected by reference headers (FOLDOC, 2000). Within each thread are individual postings. Both threads and postings can be considered units of conversational analysis. Analyzing a conversation may begin by simply quantifying the following: Number of participants, number of levels in the thread, number of entries per participant, and length of each entry.

Each discussion will be different; however, it seems useful to suggest common dimensions that could be used to analyze online discussions. These dimensions may include the characteristics of participants, of the discussion group, and of the particular discussion itself.

Participant Characteristics

Personal disclosure. It is possible to disguise online identity completely or to divulge a great deal. Domain names can indicate whether the participant is from a particular university or company. Hotmail accounts reveal little, and some services actually strip all identification and allow complete anonymity. An Aol.com address inadvertently reveals new user status. Actual names–"John Smythe" rather than handles "nospamJohn"–provide the same identity online as in the physical world.

Expertise. Participants can establish expertise by their use of terminology, abbreviations, etc. Famously, Usenet hacker group participants provide a hack in their messages. A reputation for expertise can be established over time.

Motivation for response. It is useful to consider what participants want out of the discussion. They may just want to be entertained or to feel a part of a group. They also may be motivated to persuade, to win, or to dominate or to vent their emotions.

Perspective. Participants bring the same biases online that exist in the real world. Gender, race, ethnicity, SES, and occupation all influence their contributions. Perspective may sometimes be inferred from the discussion group itself.

Sample. Respondents may or may not be representative of some population, and the observer may or may not be able to know this fact.

Message Characteristics

Message tone. Tone refers to the participants' attitudes toward other participants and toward the subject matter. Tone is often a direct reflection of the motivation of participants. Referring to other members by their first names, using slang, incomplete sentences, for example, indicate a less formal tone.

Conflict. This refers to clear differences of opinion. Independent of whether conflicting views are expressed, messages differ in the extent to which other members are treated with respect. At the extreme opposite end of the spectrum, participants may engage in deliberate insults known as "flame wars." Online emotion is generally expressed through word choice, and it can be confounded with civility. Exclamation points and other expressions, ☺ ☹ can be used to substitute for voice inflection.

Specific terminology and themes. Perhaps most importantly, discussions can be characterized by the particular terms used and points made. These terms are used to compile a dictionary that can be used in content analysis. Online discussion content analysis can quantify these terms and topics using commercially available software (Popping 1997).

THE CASE OF NIKE LABOR PRACTICES: TWO DISCUSSIONS

This section applies the criteria above to two discussions, chosen to illustrate views concerning labor practices in factories that manufacture Nike products (cf. Kahle, Boush, and Phelps 2000). Such discussions may be useful to academics interested in opinion toward business and economic globalization and to particular companies such as Nike.

Usenet Group rec.sport.golf

The first discussion, Usenet group rec.sport.golf, was found using the topic search on the website *www.deja.com* (now part of *google.com*), which organizes Usenet bulletin boards. The search "Nike and workers" revealed a number of discussions, one of which criticized Tiger Woods and Nike for underpaying workers in Thailand who make Nike products. Usenet organizes the discussion threads, making it easy to trace the flow of a discussion (see Figure 1). A partial verbatim is included as Figure 2 and discussed below (see Figure 2).

Participant Characteristics

Personal disclosure. All four participants appeared to be using their real names. (Last names were deleted here, and email addresses slightly

FIGURE 1. Thread of Usenet Group rec.sport.golf–Subject Tiger $$$$

Message	Author	Date
Msg 1	Marc	11/15/2000
Msg 2	Tom	11/15/2000
Msg 3	Marc	11/15/2000
Msg 4	Harlan	11/15/2000
Msg 5	Marc	11/15/2000
Msg 6	Annika 1980	11/15/2000
Msg 7	Marc	11/15/2000
Msg 8	Bruce	11/15/2000
Msg 9	George	11/15/2000
Msg 10	Greenbud	11/16/2000
Msg 11	John J.	11/26/2000
Msg 12	George	11/26/2000
Msg 13	jowall	11/27/2000
Msg 14	jowall	11/15/2000
Msg 15	Mark	11/15/2000
Msg 16	O'B	11/15/2000
Msg 17	zig	11/15/2000
Msg 18	Matt	11/16/2000

FIGURE 2. Tiger $$$$ Partial Thread, Verbatim

Message 1

Author: Marc <nospammarc@hotmail.com>

Did you know that Tiger gets paid, for one day, the equivalent of 14,000 Nike "employees" in Thailand.
    Boycott Nike at Xmas !!!!!

Message 2

Author: Tom <tom@attglobal.net>

Why just Christmas?

Message 3

Author: Marc <nospammarc@hotmail.com>

Agree. I have boycotted Nike for 2 years now......

Message 4

Author: Harlan <h@ntsource.com>

Well, Marc, your boycott doesn't seem to have worked, and I suspect one of the reasons it hasn't worked is because those people in Thailand need the money...however little it might seem to you. They may work for peanuts in Thailand, but it also costs them fewer peanuts to buy what they need. Which culture are you comparing them to? Each culture has its own needs, laws and mores. I'm not sure those people working for peanuts really appreciate your attempt to take their jobs away. Its up to the Thais to regulate their own economic system, pass their own child labor laws, etc.

Its your right to protest through boycott, and I hope it works, because it means the jobs will be that much closer to coming back to the U.S. But don't expect unrealistic results in the short term. And if it does work, how many of those Thai people/kids will be out picking garbage out of dumps instead of working in what you may consider a sweatshop. Ever been to Thailand?
    Just my opinion.
    Harlan

Message 5

Author: Marc <nospammarc@hotmail.com>

To give Tiger 100 million US dollars is criminal and obscene. Give him a million a year, and give these slaves a little more than 20 cents an hour, 80 hour weeks. No lunch or pee breaks. My God man, I hope you realize that youwon the lottery on the day you were born.

Sure, I can't change the world, but, by Chri.. (oops, no swearing), I just might change just a little bit of it. Not buying $10 sneakers for $200 just might help. Hey, I can be idealistic, after all, I am a former flower child, now retired and returning to the ideals of the 60's

Message 18

Author: Matt <Matt@pacifier.com>

Funny, you seem to be comparing the US money value to Thailand money value. oh boo hoo, that Nike worker in Thailand only gets $.05 American dollars....Wait that $.05 is equal to 2.19 Baht....gee that sure is comparable to any other worker in Thailand gets from other Thai company. Morons like you should study things before opening your mouth.

altered to maintain anonymity). Based on the first names they are all male.

Expertise. There are few signs of genuine expertise in this area, although the tone of the arguments indicates a reasonably high level of education, as does the vocabulary and spelling. We actually do not know whether one or more of the participants has a stake for or against Nike.

Motivation for response. Participants presumably just want to sound off. We have little reason to believe that participants have a strong motivation to remain a member in good standing of the loose and transitive community represented by a golf discussion group. We see at least some indication of a desire to persuade. As suggested above, one or more participants may be anti-Nike activists.

Message Characteristics

Formality. The arguments by Harlan and Matt have a rather formal complete structure. Participants are informal in addressing each other.

Civility. The level of civility ranges greatly. Harlan ends his entry with the self-effacing "Just my opinion." Matt ends his entry with a sentence that includes "Morons like you."

Conflict. The entire discussion is characterized by high conflict. Even Tom, who seems to agree with Marc, the initiator of this part of the thread, couches his agreement that Nike should be boycotted with the somewhat challenging "Why just Christmas?"

Emotion. Word choice seems to suggest a moderately high level of emotion.

Specific terminology and themes. Some dictionary terms suggested by this thread would include "sweatshop," "boycott," "working for peanuts," and "slaves."

www.razzberry.com

The second discussion was located by searching the search engine *www.google.com* using the same words "Nike and workers." This led to a discussion on the opinion site *www.razzberry.com*, which is affiliated with the site *www.chickclick.com*. The latter's self-described target is females ages 12-29. The thread of the discussion is not as explicitly traced as in a Usenet group. A partial list of verbatim responses is shown in Figure 3 and discussed as follows.

FIGURE 3. Partial Verbatim Discussion Concerning Nike
www.razzberry.com

sweatshops
razz from Rhain

I hate Nike straight out. Why? It's not that I hate the name or anything it is how they treat their workers and how they pay them. They pay thier workers 20 cents an hour, and a little under two dollars a day. That is not enough to for the workers to buy food! They also abuse the workers. They touch, hit, and make unwanted sexual advances on the women. As women shouldn't we try to do something about this? Please air your views on this company and the other companiess that use sweatshops.

Tweety m. wrote on 5/15/99 12:45:06 PM [mst]:
I personally think that If everyone knows how Nike is treating there workers than something must be done about it. Like a boycott of there products or something of that sort. But the other thing is that alot of people don't really know what is going on I found out just know by reding this article and I know from know on I won't be buying Nike anymore

---

HEX (hex69ing) wrote on 5/11/99 12:47:05 PM [mst]:
I think its unfair to the hard working men woman and children that tha get abused and misstreated but i dont want nike to move thare factory's because then that 2 $ a day would go to nothing and it harder to get food with no money at least this way thay get some. i think that nike should protect it workers some how (i dont know how!) but i also think that boycotting nike because thay under pay there workers is worong just look at it like thisthay sell 100 shoes, if you boycott thay sell 75.if each pair costes $100.00 than you stop $2500.00 from getin to the workers and thay fire some of them. So in turn your not hurting nike but the people how work for them, understand??? Its like you trying to help by boycotting them just made the problem that much worrs.

SRunyan279 wrote on 5/11/99 5:02:46 AM [mst]:
I'm glad someone said somethinh about this! I've never bought a Nike product in my life! Plus, Nike's pretty much out of style anyways!

Katie wrote on 5/10/99 2:16:03 PM [mst]:
I hate Nike...they treat people like they are non-human...my boyfriend has an Anti-Nike shirt...its real cool....I know for a fact that Nike isnt the only one...

Participant Characteristics

Personal disclosure. There is little personal disclosure, either in the domain names of their e-mail addresses or in given names. Participants use handles, such as "Tweety," although presumably "Katie" is a real first name and "Runyan" is probably a real last name. For some purposes, the handle "hex69ing" would constitute a kind of self-disclosure, although possibly more indicative of a desire for a different online persona than a reflection of the real one.

Expertise. There are few facts of any kind anywhere in this discussion. Rhain, who started the discussion, notes that Nike pays its workers 20 cents an hour. It is more notable what facts are not mentioned, for example, that this pay varies by country because standards differ by country and that Nike itself does not own the factories.

Motivation for response. The purpose seems to be to connect with others on this issue and perhaps to share common feelings. Hex is at least partly motivated to persuade.

Perspective. The perspective is revealed most clearly in the initial posting by Rhain in the phrase "As women shouldn't we try to do something about this?"

Message Characteristics

Formality. The language is informal. Participants use contractions ("won't"), slang ("real cool"), and sentences sometimes run on or are incomplete.

Conflict. The only conflict expressed comes from Hex. All others agree with all the basic premises and conclusions. Katie's final comment "I know that Nike isn't the only one" flies directly in the face of agreeing with a Nike boycott; however, the high need to go along may cause this thought to be couched as agreement.

Civility. Participants are extremely civil toward one another. The conflict expressed by Hex makes no direct criticism of other participants and includes terms such as "I think" and "I don't know how!" to soften the conflict of her entry.

Emotion. Emotion runs fairly high throughout, probably because of the tone of the initial posting. Three of the five entries include exclamation points.

Terminology and themes. Terms for a content analysis dictionary would include "sweatshops," "boycotting," "women," "children," "unwanted sexual advances," "out of style," "non-human."

Overall Interpretation of the Nike Discussions

Overall, the Usenet discussion indicates a high level of conflict, a wide range of civility, and high levels of both emotion and reasoned argument. The conversation among younger women indicates a low level of conflict, notable civility, and more emotion than specific arguments. One interesting notion that occurs twice is the confounding of fashion with social issues. SRunyan279 notes that "Nike's pretty much out of style anyways!" and Katie refers to her boyfriend's anti-Nike shirt as "real cool." For both academics and practitioners, this discussion yields interesting hypotheses about influences of social awareness on product perception and vice versa. The discussion also reveals the precise wording of spontaneous consumer conversation about Nike. More specifically for Nike, consumers in the discussion among younger women express disturbing impressions of Nike's treatment of women. An interesting implication for WOL is that online groups such as these may be influencing a much larger number of non-participants (lurkers). Recent research indicates that the degree to which these kinds of negative comments influence opinion is affected by attributions (Laczniak, DeCarlo, and Ramaswami, 2001). When negative comments are attributed to the brand (in this case Nike), brand evaluations decrease. However, when negative comments are attributed to the communicator, brand evaluations increase. This may indicate that there sometimes may be a backlash against negative word-of-mouth.

Qualitative interpretation such as is described above may lead to interesting hypotheses about how particular groups of people think about Nike, but they are subject to the same biases as focus groups and other qualitative techniques. Therefore, one approach would be to use online discussions as a first stage in research, to be followed by survey research using a representative sample of Nike consumers. However, it is possible to quantify online opinion without recourse to surveys. The next section discusses some of the issues related to such measurement.

QUANTITATIVE CONTENT ANALYSIS

Presumably consumers have some base level of animosity toward Nike and most other companies. Managers may actually take counterproductive actions if they believe erroneously that consumers are displeased with their products or actions. Therefore it makes sense to quantify the negative sentiment expressed.

The first question is "what should we count?" Previous research usually emphasizes a distinction between concepts and relationships. Text analysis can be classified as either thematic or relational (Roberts 1997). Thematic text analysis is concerned with occurrences (or counts) of *concepts*. In the current context, it may be instructive to count the incidence of phrases such as "I hate Nike" or "boycott Nike." Relational text analysis is concerned with the *relationships* among concepts. Key relationships could involve effects of attitudes on each other and on behavior. For example, we might map (and count) relationships among the following concepts: "Nike workers are underpaid," "Nike athletes are overpaid," "Nike products are overpriced," and "I will not buy Nike products."

Perhaps the next question is "what content?" It is impossible to analyze all online discussion group content on any subject, so some sampling decisions are necessary. The population from which the sample is taken will be dictated by the purpose of the research. In the current example Nike may be interested in the opinions only of those participating in a particular sport or in a particular demographic range. If discussion groups are organized by interest area they may not correspond to a target market profile. The sampling process itself will probably involve multiple stages. Some subset of discussion groups will be chosen and then some subset of discussion content or threads will be chosen. Choice of discussion groups may begin by choosing search engines.

Finally, we need to consider how the data can be analyzed. The analyses will be dominated by the comparisons that are made. If the purpose is to determine whether attitudes toward Nike are worsening, the comparison would be across time. For example we could examine whether there is a trend in the incidence of negative statements about Nike. Similarly, a comparison may be made in response to a particular event, such as a media report or public demonstration. More general comparisons of interest to academics include comparisons across domain types (Nike vs. Major League Baseball), comparisons across levels of analysis (organizations vs. issues), comparisons between consumer groups, and comparisons between discussion groups and different media (websites, search engine results).

If attitudes toward Nike are indeed worsening, is it advantageous for Nike to take action? To a large extent the answer depends on the consequences of taking action or failing to take action. This can be addressed by signal detection theory, which we explore in the next section.

SIGNAL DETECTION THEORY

Signal detection theory (Smith and Wilson, 1953; Tanner and Swets, 1954) provides a method for interpreting ambiguously intense stimuli. Before people can respond to a stimulus, they must perceive that it exists and interpret its meaning. The stimulus intensity must surpass the minimum intensity to register with the central nervous system. For example, if a very faint whisper-like sound is in the air, the listener must decide whether the sound is ambient white noise, a trick of the listener's own central nervous system, or in fact a real whisper. As applied to on-line data, a signal may consist of consumer discontent or of a particular consumer belief. Signal detection theory may be helpful in determining whether the expression of such beliefs is more than ambient noise.

We will focus our discussion here on a few aspects of signal detection theory. The main concepts we will try to apply are the "likelihood ratio," and the decision "criterion." The likelihood ratio is the fundamental computation involved in deciding whether or not a signal actually occurred. This decision is biased, however, by the consequences of the decision and by the a priori likelihood of a signal occurring. The decision consequences and the a priori likelihood combine to determine the "criterion" for deciding whether a signal has occurred. Observation is compared with the criterion, and then a decision results as to whether there really was a signal. A more precise description follows, along with a description of how each concept may be applied to the Nike case.

Likelihood Ratio

Two probabilities are relevant to signal detection: (1) the probability that if a signal had been present the signal would have occurred, and (2) the probability that the observed sensory input would have occurred if no signal had been present. The first probability divided by the second probability is the *likelihood ratio* for detecting the signal. Essentially it represents the ratio between a true positive signal detection and a false positive.

In deciding whether consumers are truly discontented with Nike labor practices we should consider both probabilities involved in the likelihood ratio. The first probability may be estimated by counting the incidence of key words or phrases in online discussion groups. The likelihood of capturing a fair representation of such discussion groups would be affected by the number and comprehensiveness of search engines. In addition, the key words used in these searches would need to be comprehensive and consistent over time. Once identified, discussions could be analyzed using content analysis software (e.g., NUD*IST). A qualitative analysis as described earlier could be used to develop the "dictionary" of terms for the content analysis.

The probability of false positives is affected by at least two kinds of online discussion responses. One is that non-consumers such as political activists may be the source of some discussion comments. The other is that competitors may actually plant discussions as a way to sabotage company efforts. In both cases, the remedy seems to be control or management of discussion participants.

Criterion

Detecting a stimulus is not merely a physiological process–it also involves the psychological consequences of detecting one thing or another. For example, presentation of an obscene word requires a greater intensity to be "detected" than of a neutral word, presumably because the embarrassment of detecting an obscene message incorrectly raises the required certainty for interpreting the sound. The perceiver must determine the potential consequences in terms of potential costs and rewards for detecting or not detecting a signal. This "payoff matrix" of costs and rewards is one of the main determinants of the criterion used to decide whether a signal has actually occurred.

In the current context, the consequences of detecting a marketing-related signal may involve profit and loss. The payoff matrix will vary not only by company, but also by the particular signal under consideration (see Table 1).

This matrix will determine which signals are worth seeking. For example, Nike may face a very symmetrical payoff matrix for the signal that "Nike abuses workers." That is, the penalty is the same for a mistaken positive decision as for a mistaken negative one. Or Nike managers may decide that no marketing action would be forthcoming regardless of the signal that was detected. The payoff matrices are likely to be different for different kinds of negative signals. For example, the payoff matrix for the signal "Nike products are unfashionable" may have a much more interesting payoff matrix because it would involve changes in product lines. The point is that the payoffs for detecting each particular kind of signal have to be considered as an integral part of the analysis.

TABLE 1. Example Payoff Matrix for the Signal "Nike Abuses Workers"

	Signal Present	Signal Absent
Signal Detected	Nike benefits from needed public relations campaign.	Nike wastes resources on unnecessary public relations campaign.
Signal Not Detected	Nike name is eroded because of inaction to counter negative attitudes.	Nike benefits by ignoring meaningless "noise" concerning human rights policies.

REFERENCES

Fox, Nick and Chris Roberts (1999). GPs in Cyberspace: The Sociology of a Virtual Community. *The Sociological Review*, 47 (November), 643-671.

Free Online Dictionary of Computing (FOLDOC), Updated July 12, 2000 *http: //foldoc.doc.ic.ac.uk/foldoc/index.html*

Granitz, Neil A. and James C. and Ward (1996). Virtual Community: A Sociocognitive Analysis. *Advances in Consumer Research*, 23, 161-166.

Hagel, John III and Arthur Armstrong (1997), *Net Gain: Expanding Markets Through Virtual Communities*, Cambridge: HBS Press.

Jones, S.G. (1995). "Understanding Computers in the Information Age." In *Cybersociety: Computer-Mediated Communication and Community*, S.G. Jones, Ed., London: Sage.

Kahle, Lynn R., David M. Boush, and Mark Phelps. (2000). Good Morning, Vietnam: An Ethical Analysis of Nike Activities in Southeast Asia. *Sport Marketing Quarterly*, 9 (1), 43-52.

Katona, George, and Eva Mueller (1955). "A Study of Purchase Decisions." In *The Dynamics of Consumer Reaction*, Lincoln H. Clark, Ed., New York: New York University Press, 30-87.

Kollock, Peter, and Marc A. Smith (1999). "Communities in Cyberspace." In *Communities in Cyberspace*, Marc A. Smith and Peter Kollock, Eds., London: Routledge, 3-25.

Lasswell, H.D. (1948). "The Structure and Function of Communication in Society." In *The Communication of Ideas*, L. Bryson, Ed., New York: Harper and Rowe, 37-51.

Laczniak, Russell N., Thomas E. DeCarlo, and Sridhar N. Ramaswami (2001). Consumers' Responses to Negative Word-of-Mouth Communication: An Attribution Theory Perspective. *Journal of Consumer Psychology*, 11 (1), 57-73.

Popping, Roel (1997). "Computer Programs for the Analysis of Texts." In *Text Analysis for the Social Sciences: Methods for Drawing Statistical Inferences from Texts and Transcripts*, Carl W. Roberts, Ed., Mahwah, NJ: Lawrence Erlbaum Associates, Inc., 209-221.

Rheingold, H. (1993). *The Virtual Community*, New York: Addison-Wesley.

Richins, Marsha L. (1983). Negative Word of Mouth by Dissatisfied Consumers: A Pilot Study. *Journal of Marketing*, 47 (1), 68-78.

Roberts, Carl W. (1997). "A Theoretical Map for Selecting Among Text Analysis Methods." In *Text Analysis for the Social Sciences: Methods for Drawing Statistical Inferences from Texts and Transcripts*, Carl W. Roberts, Ed., Mahwah, NJ: Lawrence Erlbaum Associates, Inc., 275-283.

Smith, M. and E. Wilson (1953). A Model of Auditory Threshold and Its Application to the Problem of the Multiple Observer. *Psychological Monographs*, 67 (9), 1-35.

Smith, Robert E. and Christine A. Vogt (1995). The Effects of Integrating Advertising and Negative Word of Mouth Communication on Message Processing and Response. *Journal of Consumer Psychology*, 4 (2), 133-151.

Stewart, David W. and Michael A. Kamins (1993). *Secondary Information Sources and Methods*, 2nd ed., Newbury Park, CA: Sage Publications.

Tanner, W. P. and J. A. Swets (1954). A Decision-Making Theory of Visual Detection. *Psychological Review*, 61, 401-409.

Index

Printed in the United States
by Baker & Taylor Publisher Services